D1243893

THE
STRUCTURED
COBOLER'S GUIDE

THE
STRUCTURED
COBOLER'S GUIDE

THAYNE A. SHANK

Federal Express Corporation

Systems Integration

PRENTICE-HALL, INC., Englewood Cliffs, New Jersey 07632

Overize
QA 76
.73
.C25
S39
1984

Library of Congress Cataloging in Publication Data

Shank, Thayne A. (date)
  The structured coboler's guide.

  1. COBOL (Computer program language) 2. Structured
programming. I. Title.
QA76.73.C25S39 1984   001.64'24   83-4446
ISBN 0-13-854448-4

Editorial/production supervision and interior design: Joan Foley
Cover design: Ray Lundgren
Manufacturing buyer: Ed O'Dougherty

© 1984 by Prentice-Hall, Inc., Englewood Cliffs, New Jersey 07632

All rights reserved. No part of this book may be
reproduced, in any form or by any means,
without permission in writing from the publisher.

Printed in the United States of America

10 9 8 7 6 5 4 3 2 1

ISBN 0-13-854448-4

H372772
bc

Prentice-Hall International, Inc., London
Prentice-Hall of Australia Pty. Limited, Sydney
Editora Prentice-Hall do Brasil, Ltda., Rio de Janeiro
Prentice-Hall Canada Inc., Toronto
Prentice-Hall of India Private Limited, New Delhi
Prentice-Hall of Japan, Inc., Tokyo
Prentice-Hall of Southeast Asia Pte. Ltd., Singapore
Whitehall Books Limited, Wellington, New Zealand

TO MOM AND DAD

WITH ALL MY LOVE

514045

VISUAL TABLE OF CONTENTS

```
                    ┌──────────────────┐
                    │       THE        │
                    │    STRUCTURED    │
                    │    COBOLER'S      │
                    │     GUIDE        │
                    └────────┬─────────┘
        ┌────────────┬───────┴────────┬─────────────────┐
   ┌────┴────┐  ┌────┴────┐     ┌─────┴─────┐    ┌───────┴──────┐
   │  VTOCs   │  │ HIPOs   │     │PROGRAMMING│    │ PUTTING IT   │
   │   1.0    │  │  2.0    │     │    3.0    │    │ ALL TOGETHER │
   └────┬─────┘  └────┬────┘     └─────┬─────┘    │     4.0      │
        │             │                │          └───────┬──────┘
```

VISUAL TABLE OF CONTENTS

CONTENTS

PREFACE

VTOCs 1.0

CONCEPTS

METHODOLOGY 1.1

EXAMPLES

A VTOC

PRIMARY PRINCIPLES OF DESIGN

TWO TYPES OF VTOCs

TWO OBSERVATIONS

SECONDARY PRINCIPLES OF DESIGN

HIPOs 2.0

CONCEPTS

METHODOLOGY AND EXAMPLES

PROGRAMMING 3.0

CONCEPTS AND METHODOLOGY

EXAMPLES

PUTTING IT ALL TOGETHER 4.0

EXAMPLES

STRUCTURED TESTING

STRUCTURED WALK-THRUS

STANDARDS MANUAL

CONTENTS

PREFACE

This handbook was developed to be an aid in giving programmers and analysts the ability to create and code COBOL programs directly from the structured design tools: Visual Table of Contents Charts (VTOCs), and Hierarchical Input Process Output Charts (HIPOs). A methodology will also be developed that allows the programmer to code structured COBOL programs "on the fly" without designing them.

It is also assumed the reader understands that the majority of the work published and lectured on about the structured methodologies was and is for the purpose of monetary gain and fame. (Corollary: "If you take it all too seriously, I have a bridge you can buy," or Shank's Law: "Ninety percent of all structured COBOL programs is FILLER.")

ACKNOWLEDGMENTS

"Business Systems Planning, Information Systems Planning Guide" Second Edition (October 1978), IBM Corporation, Technical Publications, Dept. 824, 1122 Westchester Avenue, White Plains, New York 10604.

"Structured Design" by Ed Yourdon and Larry L. Constantine, copyright 1975, Edward Yourdon and Larry L. Constantine, Yourdon Inc., 1133 Avenue of the Americas, New York, New York 10036.

SPECIAL THANKS

Cynthia Dyer for all the illustrations and art work.

Pam Fager, and my wife, Kay, for all the rest of the hard work.

CONCEPTS

Visual Table of Contents (VTOCs) are probably the best structured tool available for designing systems and programs if used correctly. They incorporate four primary principles of design: top-down, modularity, functional decomposition and user involvement.

There are two types of VTOCs (although most authors use only one): structural and procedural. A structural VTOC depicts the functions of a system/program without implying in what order they should be executed (e.g., a blueprint of a building), while a procedural VTOC combines the functions with procedure, which shows not only the functions but also the order of execution (e.g., the blueprint plus construction plans).

In designing systems and programs using VTOCs, four secondary principles of design should be observed: 1. High cohesion (the inter-relatedness of each module), 2. Low coupling (independency between modules on the same level), 3. A good span of control (2-6 functions within each module), 4. The right amount of detail (resolves itself into 2-10 lines of code per bottom module).

We therefore have four "major" and four "minor" principles of design used in designing two types of VTOCs: structural and procedural.

1.1 METHODOLOGY

A VTOC

By first "doing" a VTOC we will be able to more easily understand the principles involved.

Assume we want to design a system that simulates the activities a person is involved in throughout a 24-hour day over the course of a year.

One approach would be the following. Our system could be called Days Activities.

```
┌──────────────┐
│    DAYS      │
│  ACTIVITIES  │
└──────────────┘
```

The box represents a module, function or process (we will use the terms as synonyms). It represents the top function of the VTOC.

We next determine what type of days make up a year. A year could be broken down several ways (months, seasons, Monday, Tuesday, Wednesday, ..., odd and even days, etc.), but for the present time we will design our second level as:

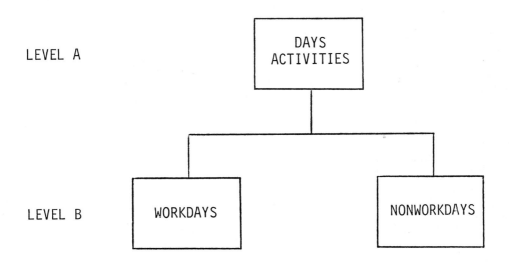

3

Decomposing <u>workdays</u>, we could have:

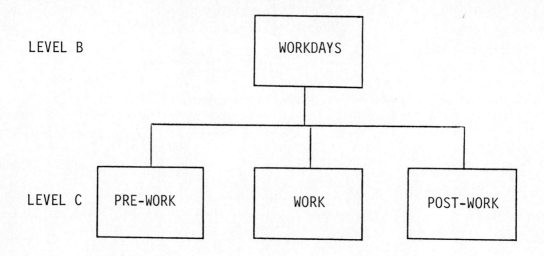

If we assume a day is from midnight to midnight, the function <u>pre-work</u> could be broken down:

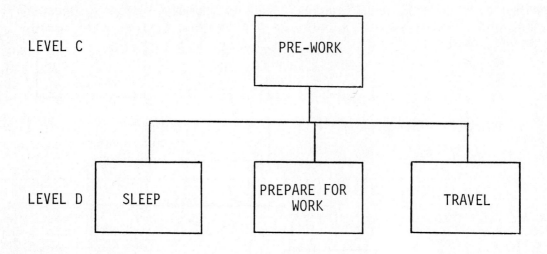

Continuing in this fashion following one branch of the VTOC, we would have:

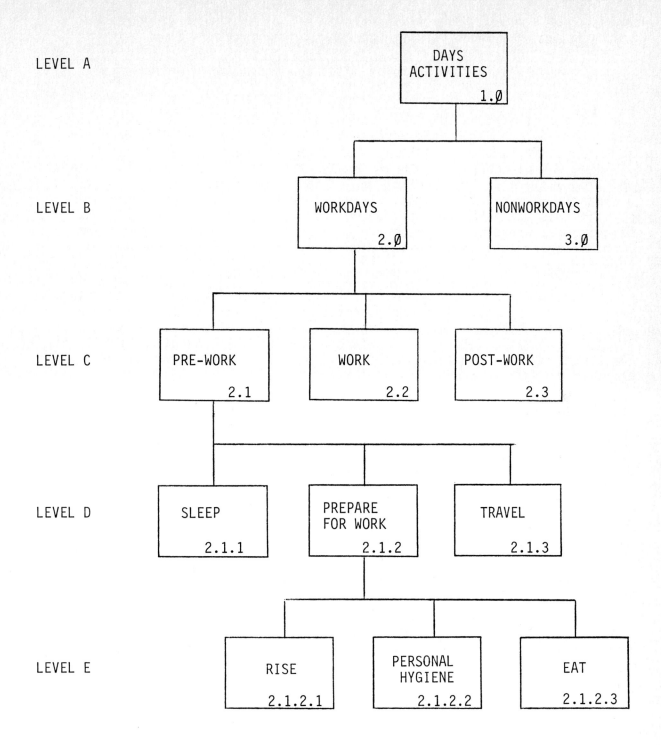

You could continue this process until you were down to the minutest detail. (For example, <u>bite into cornflake</u>.)

5

PRIMARY PRINCIPLES OF DESIGN

All of the primary principles of design are evident in our simple VTOC.

First, it is TOP-DOWN. We started at the most all-inclusive function and identified the principle functions within it. We then divided those functions into their subfunctions. This, by the way, is not the traditional way of designing programs and/or systems. Traditionally, systems and programs are designed bottom-up. This is due mainly to the fact that "DP people" are detail minded. We tend to get involved in the detail as soon as possible. We are then forced to combine the detail to get to a higher level where we combine again until we reach the apex. (This method is not completely without merit but we will restrict our discussion to top-down design.)

Second, we have designed our system using MODULES. Modules are used when you don't want to develop systems using the blob method. (The blob method, from a DPers point of view, is simply to have all of the programs for the new system written by the second week of the project and still miss the deadline for implementation by $2\frac{1}{2}$ years.) Using modules, you break the problem down into well-defined small pieces.

Each module (function, process or box) will become a system, subsystem, program, paragraph or part of a paragraph in the new system.

Third, we developed our design by FUNCTIONALLY DECOMPOSING each module into the functions that make it up. We have not determined yet what makes a good module or why we chose the modules we did. (This will be covered under "Secondary Principles of Design.") At this time the most important issue is to be sure that each function is totally explained by the function which comprises it (e.g., workdays + nonworkdays = days' activities, with nothing left over).

The fourth "primary principle of design" is USER INVOLVEMENT. This is accomplished by using "functions" to design our system. Entire systems can be designed by adhering to terminology (functions) that users understand. You do not have to mention programs, sorts, bytes, bits, nibbles or bi-synchronous during the design stage. Of course, the trick is turning these boxes into systems, subsystems, programs, paragraphs and pieces of paragraphs after the design is complete (which we will do).

6

TWO TYPES OF VTOCS

The "Days Activities" VTOC we designed is a structural VTOC. It only shows the functions we need in our system; it does not imply order of execution (procedure).

Two steps are needed to turn a structural VTOC into a procedural VTOC.

A) Line up the functions left to right in the order you think they should be executed (which we have already done), and

B) put conditions on the functions to control the execution of the functions.

Back to our system, take the top box (function, process, or module).

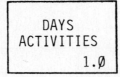

Ask yourself the question, under what circumstance do I want to or not want to execute this process. The only one I can think of is IF ALIVE!

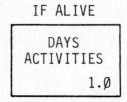

Going down to level B, a procedural VTOC might look like:

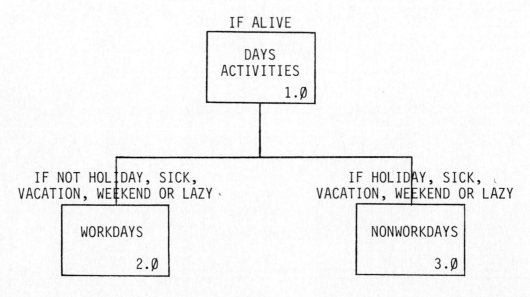

Repeating the process of putting conditions on processes, you will eventually end up with a procedural VTOC. Good system design generally dictates developing a structural VTOC first and then making it procedural.

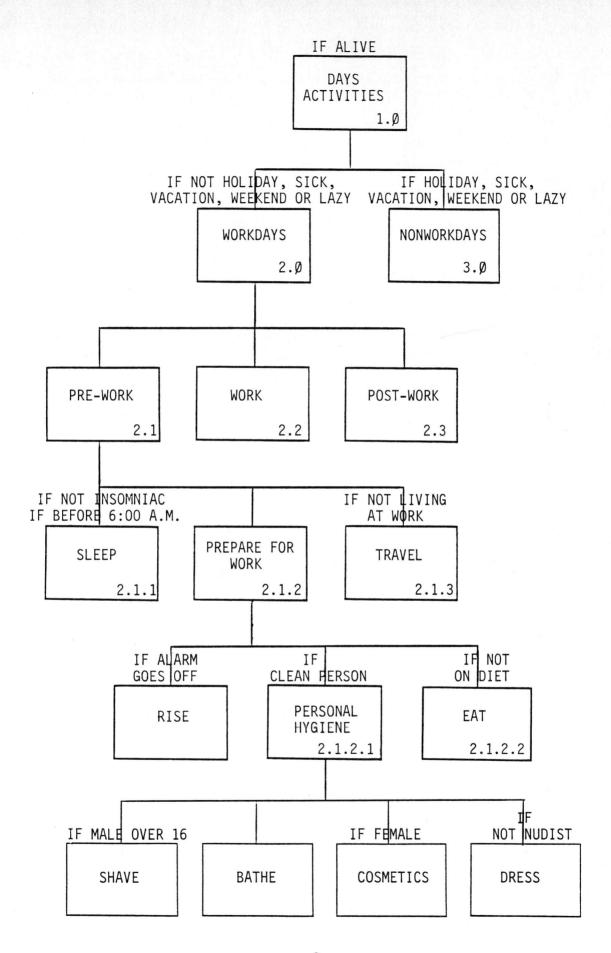

TWO OBSERVATIONS

Two observations should be made at this time since we have completed a branch of our procedural VTOC.

First, all procedural VTOCs are read top-down left to right. From days activities to workdays to pre-work to sleep to prepare for work to rise to personal hygiene to shave to bathe to cosmetics to dress to eat to travel to work to post-work to nonworkdays. That is the order (procedure) in which the functions would be executed when you have a procedural VTOC. Remember, structural VTOCs have no implied order of execution.

Second, notice that all functions which are further decomposed have no executable code; they are merely labels identifying the process. Executable code is reached only when you arrive at the functions which are not decomposed. For instance, when days activities is processed, nothing happens because it is just the name of the system.

If sleep is not broken down further, it becomes the first function which has executable code. Then you rise, then shave, then bathe and so on.

In fact, we will find out how these functions (boxes, modules, or processes) become systems, subsystems, programs, paragraphs in programs, and pieces of paragraphs. In our days activities the functions shave, bathe, cosmetics, and dress become the four components of the COBOL paragraph personal hygiene.

Rise, personal hygiene, and eat become components of the paragraph or program called prepare for work and so on, until you reach the system level of days activities.

Therefore, each function that is further decomposed becomes names of systems, subsystems (more than one program), programs and paragraph names. Functions which are not decomposed become parts of paragraphs and they contain the actual code (algorithm) which does the work.

SECONDARY PRINCIPLES OF DESIGN

Secondary and primary principles of design differ on the following points.

Primary - easy to understand

Secondary - hard to understand

Primary - possible to implement

Secondary - impossible to implement

Primary - developed by practitioners

Secondary - developed by theoreticians

Nevertheless, secondary principles of design have some merit.

First, high cohesion. Cohesion is the measure of how tight everything hangs together in a box, how closely the various pieces are related within a function, or a measure of how strong the glue is that holds the box (function, module, process) together.

The theoreticians maintain that when we group something together and give it a name we consciously or subconsciously saw something in common between the pieces that allowed us to give one name to the whole set. (E.g., all workdays must have had something in common with each other that allowed us to group them together and call them "workdays." Likewise, the pieces that make up "travel" must have had something in common since the word travel conjures up a fairly precise set of processes that allows us, when taken together as a set, to go from home to work.)

They further maintain that up to seven reasons have been identified for what criteria we use in categorizing sets of function. In other words, there are seven reasons for how functions could be related to each other, thereby allowing us to give one name to them all.

There are in turn weak (or poor) relational criteria and strong (or good) ones.

Again, let's illustrate cohesion by using our Days Activities VTOC.

The weakest form of cohesion (i.e., a poor reason to group a set of functions together) is called <u>coincidental cohesion</u>.

This type of cohesion groups a set of functions together coincidentally, for no other reason than happenstance.

Our second level of the VTOC, instead of <u>workdays</u> and <u>nonworkdays</u>, could have decomposed into the following.

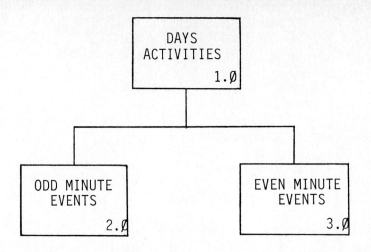

Grouping all of the functions that happen on the odd minutes of the day under one module and putting all even minute events under the other module yields coincidental cohesion.

As you can see, there will probably be no relationship between the functions identified in this matter, hence we have coincidental cohesion.

The second form of cohesion (going from weak to strong) is logical cohesion.

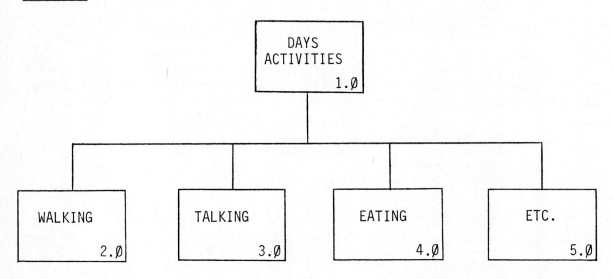

This reasoning says to group activities together that are intrinsically alike. This would obviously create a very disjunct system, causing you to jump around your VTOC in order to accomplish a simple function like "strolling through the park with your sweetie eating a hot dog".

Still, a lot of existing programs/systems use logical cohesion (e.g., the EDIT routine in a program).

Temporal cohesion is the third type of cohesion.

12

COINCIDENTAL COHESION

LOGICAL COHESION

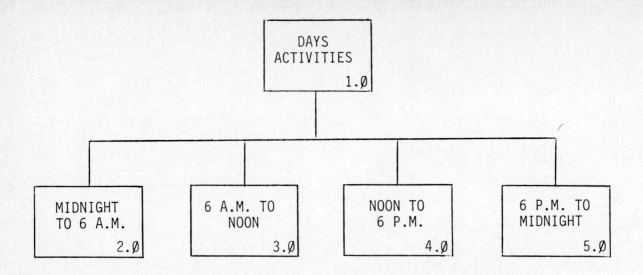

This is simply designing your systems by grouping together events that happen at approximately the same time of day. If you have ever written beginning-of-job or end-of-job routines, you are familiar with this one.

Fourth is a "toughie" called <u>procedural cohesion</u>.

TEMPORAL COHESION

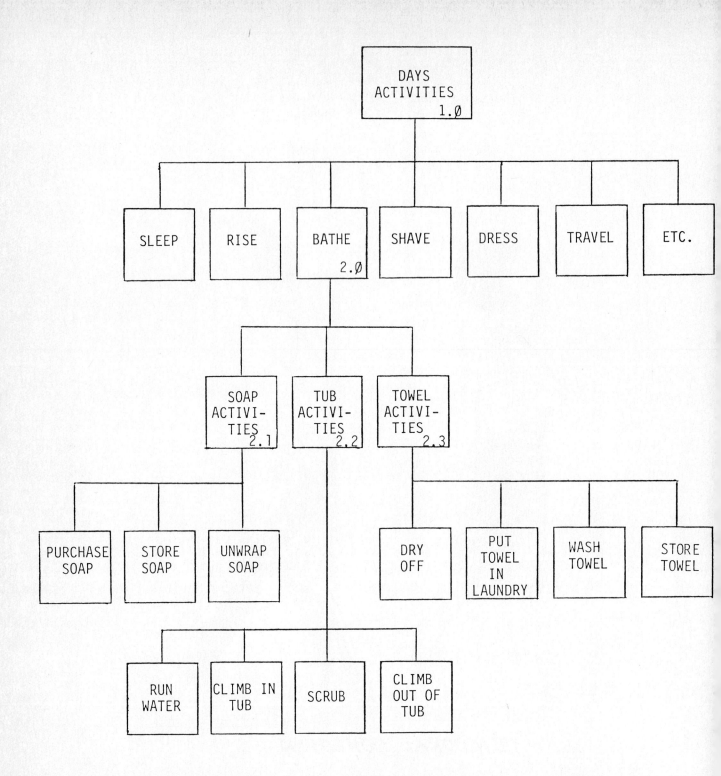

Procedural cohesion is derived by observing that a set of procedures is used to accomplish a certain task. These procedures might cross
temporal, logical, or functional lines because they include all the procedures needed to do the job.

For instance, looking at the process called bathe, it is obvious
that you have to buy and store soap, but they are not what you had in
mind when you said bathe. They are not functional; they are procedural.

Procedural cohesion includes <u>all</u> the processes necessary to accomplish the task. Many programs and systems use procedural cohesion because they are designed using flowcharts and it is very hard to determine functional divisions in a flowchart.

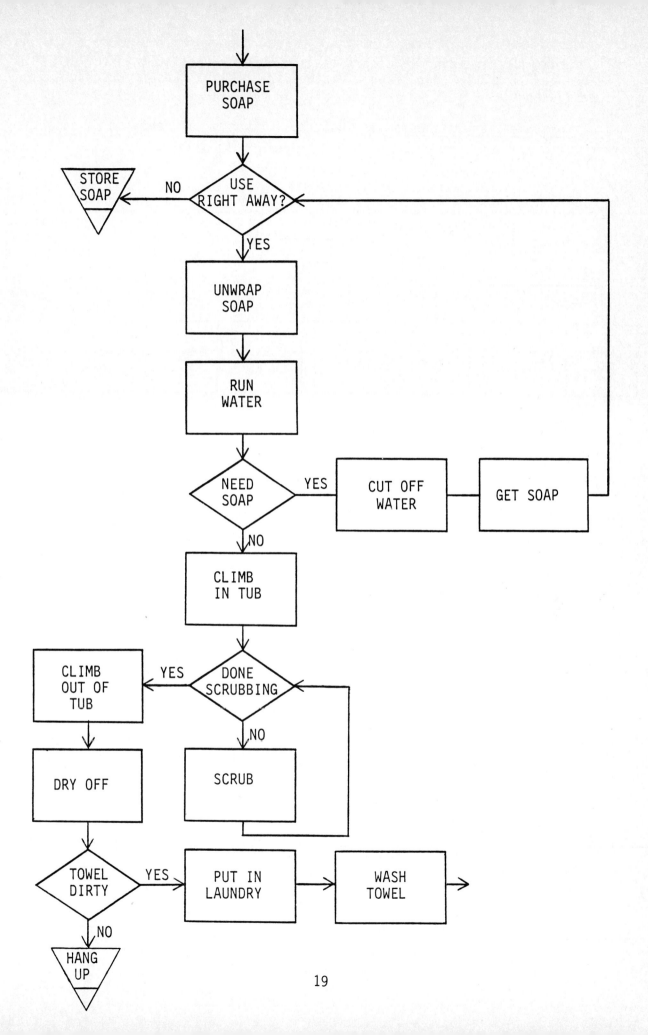

19

Using the preceding flowchart it is extremely difficult to decide where your program or paragraph divisions are, which leads to procedural cohesive modules.

Communicational cohesion is what the fifth type of cohesion is called.

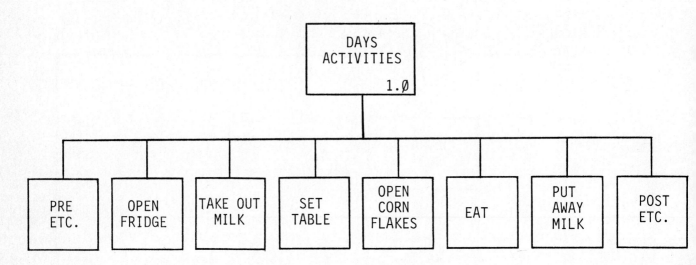

Communicational cohesion is identifying all of the processing that take place on one logical input or output record or set of data.

This can be seen more easily by using an IPO.

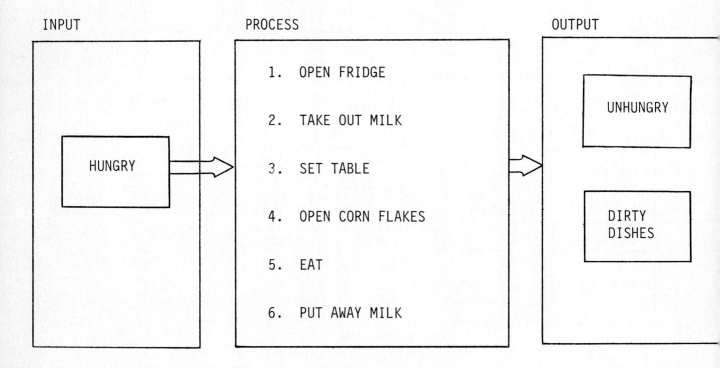

Your input record is "hungry" and you then identify all the processes you go through to process the input record. The same processes would be derived if the output record of "hungry" was used, namely "unhungry". You would then identify the processes needed to become "unhungry" and it would include the same functions as using the input record of "hungry".

Communicational cohesion is frequently encountered in system and design --- you read a record and then proceed to edit it, do calculations on it, update it and write it out.

The second strongest form of cohesion is <u>sequential cohesion</u> (so they say).

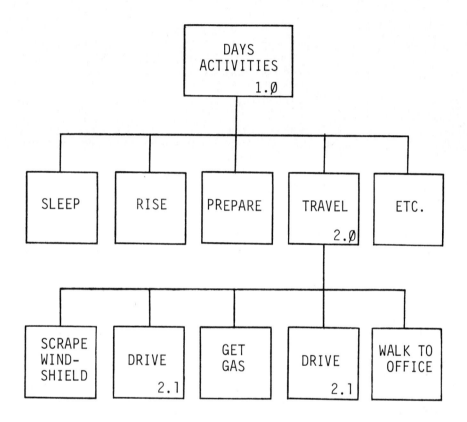

Sequential cohesion is simply observing that an output from one process generally becomes an input to another process, which in turn creates an output which becomes the input for the next process. This can be seen by using an IPO again.

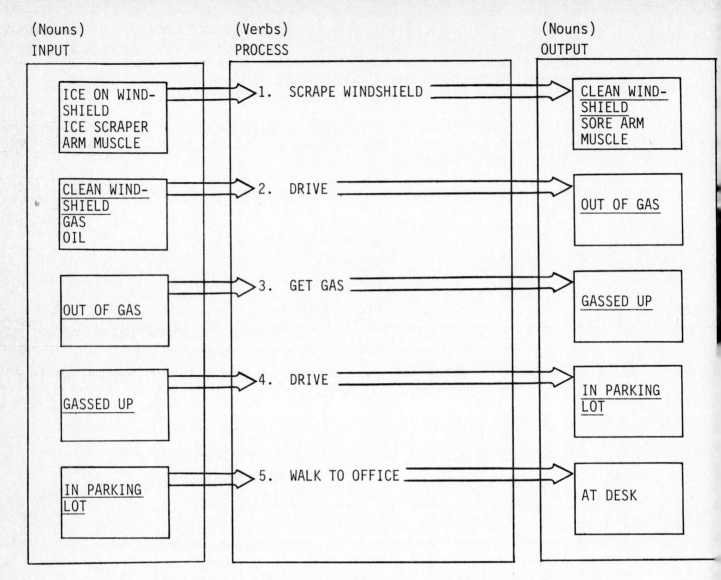

(Nouns) INPUT	(Verbs) PROCESS	(Nouns) OUTPUT
ICE ON WIND-SHIELD ICE SCRAPER ARM MUSCLE	1. SCRAPE WINDSHIELD	CLEAN WIND-SHIELD SORE ARM MUSCLE
CLEAN WIND-SHIELD GAS OIL	2. DRIVE	OUT OF GAS
OUT OF GAS	3. GET GAS	GASSED UP
GASSED UP	4. DRIVE	IN PARKING LOT
IN PARKING LOT	5. WALK TO OFFICE	AT DESK

The processes from the IPO become the processes under the function called travel. What relates them is the observation that the output from one process becomes the input to the next process.

A design created from flowcharts therefore could be predominantly sequentially cohesive.

The seventh and highest form of cohesion is called <u>functional cohesion</u>. Unfortunately the hardest cohesion to define is also functional cohesion. If you agree that darkness is the absence of light, and hate is the absence of love, and cold is the absence of heat, then this definition will be easy for you.

Functional cohesion is the absence of the first six cohesions. If this satisfies you, skip the next definition.

Functional cohesion is the cohesion you get when the USER of the system designs the system. By accepting the following corollaries, this definition makes sense.

A) Computer application systems are for the purpose of doing work normally done by <u>humans</u>.

B) The only people who know what they're doing are the <u>people</u> doing it.

C) The word <u>doing</u> could be called <u>processing</u>.

D) <u>Processing</u> is the gerund of processes which is the plural of <u>process</u>.

E) Each box on a <u>VTOC</u> is a <u>process</u>.

F) Ergo - the only way to achieve the functional cohesion is to "let the user design the system."

A further illustration might help. One reason our <u>days activities</u> system was simple to design is because we are <u>users</u>!! If we had given a robot the task of designing our system without input from humans it would have been a totally different result.

Let's assume the robot was extremely sharp (but not human), and he ended up with procedural cohesion (which is the closest cohesion to functional cohesion if all you look at is the final result).

Giving him the function called <u>bathe</u> to design, he might have ended up with the same functional decomposition we derived under our procedural cohesion section. He would have no way of knowing that some of the <u>soap activities</u> and <u>towel activities</u> were outside the function called <u>bathe</u> as far as the <u>user</u> was concerned, since <u>robots</u> don't bathe.

If he could have trimmed his <u>bathe</u> function down he would have accidentally ended up with functional cohesion. (In other words, functional cohesion is a subset of procedural cohesion.)

Lest we belabor the secondary principle of design, high cohesion, we will move on to the next secondary principle of design, low coupling and belabor it, since the first two secondary principles of design fall apart at the program level anyway.

Coupling is a measure of the dependency that each module has with other modules on the same level within the same function or with other modules within other functions. The only relationship that this definition excludes is the relationship between a function and the subfunctions under it. Getting closer to plain English we could rephrase it: can I change a module (process, function, or box) without affecting another module? If so, I have low coupling. All functions above the function changed, in the same branch, will naturally be affected.

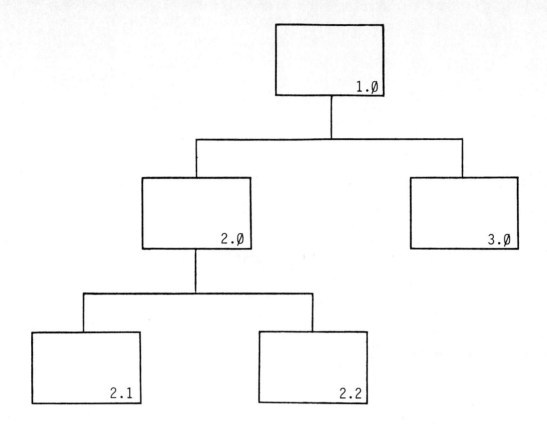

Changing 2.0 should not affect 3.0. Changing 2.2 should not affect 3.0 or 2.1, but will affect 2.0 and 1.0.

Anyone who has spent more than a week in data processing knows the consequences of high coupling. Changing one paragraph in one program in one system is tantamount to bringing the entire management information system down for the state.

Although many authors go through lengthy discussions on the different types of coupling (stamp, data, control, plus several others), I believe a rigorous analysis of coupling is less beneficial than the one we did on cohesion. If you recall, it took several pages to come to the conclusion that high cohesion is obtained by user involvement.

Cutting through this type of verbiage on coupling, I have observed two rules that, if followed, go a long way in helping obtain low coupling.

One, by keeping the conditions that control the execution of the process outside the process and two, by keeping the duplicate modules to a minimum, low coupling can be greatly enhanced.

CHANGING ONE PARAGRAPH
IN ONE PROGRAM...

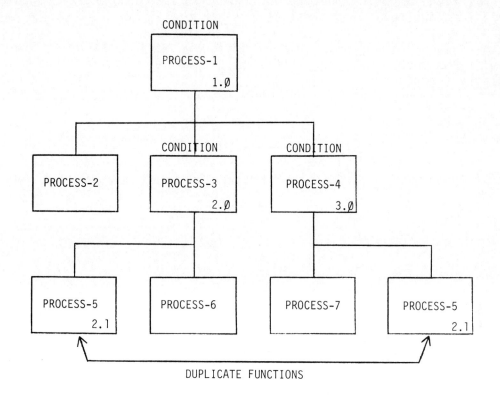

The third secondary principle of design is "span of control." It is
simply the number of functions a module is decomposed into.

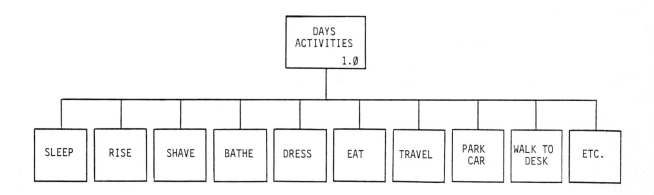

This example is logically (procedurally) correct, but there is too much detail on one level. The design takes too big a bite as far as the number of functions it handles within one function. A good rule of thumb to follow in decomposing modules is that the "span of control" should include from two to six modules.

The last secondary principle of design we will consider is used to determine how much detail our VTOC should include, "How far should I decompose my functions?"

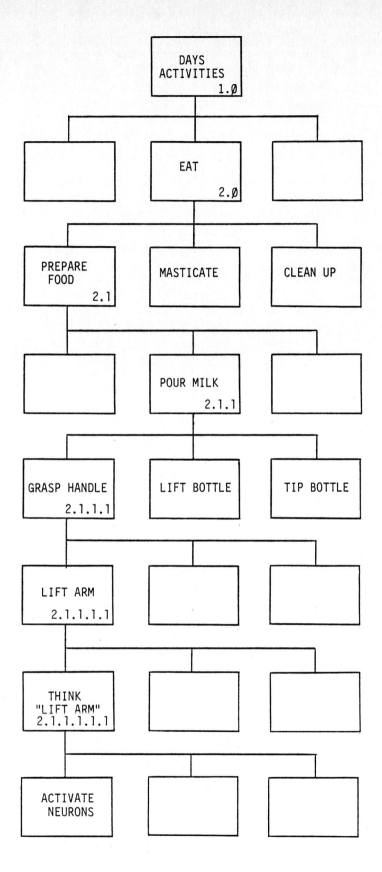

Obviously, you could decompose for quite a while, so where should you stop?

Another good rule of thumb: when you arrive at a function where you can visualize in your mind what instructions in COBOL will be needed to implement the module, STOP decomposing. Two to ten COBOL instructions will probably be the result of applying this rule. Since the bottom modules of a VTOC (those which aren't further decomposed) become parts of COBOL paragraphs, and since the span of control rule says no more than six modules should be under one function, the largest paragraph in a COBOL program will contain around fifty to sixty instructions.

Although VTOCs can be used as design tools from the highest levels of your Management Information System to the smallest algorithm, our application of VTOCs will be from the program level down.

Some parting comments before walking through an example of a program VTOC.

The VTOC as a design tool has several advantages over other design tools. It is pictorial instead of verbal. It can be procedural or structural. It can be used at all levels of systems design. It can be used with a variety of programming languages. Code can be developed directly from the VTOC. There is a one-to-one relationship between VTOCs and the three logic structures we'll cover under the programming section. It serves as good documentation. It is user oriented. It forces modular and top-down design. And finally, it is an ideal tool to use with system and program design because it is hierarchical. If you examine the complex systems that exist in the world today you will discover that the majority of them are hierarchical (top-down) in nature.

The U.S. Government:

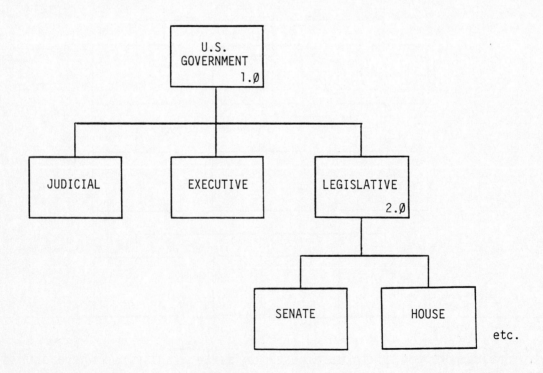

The Universe:

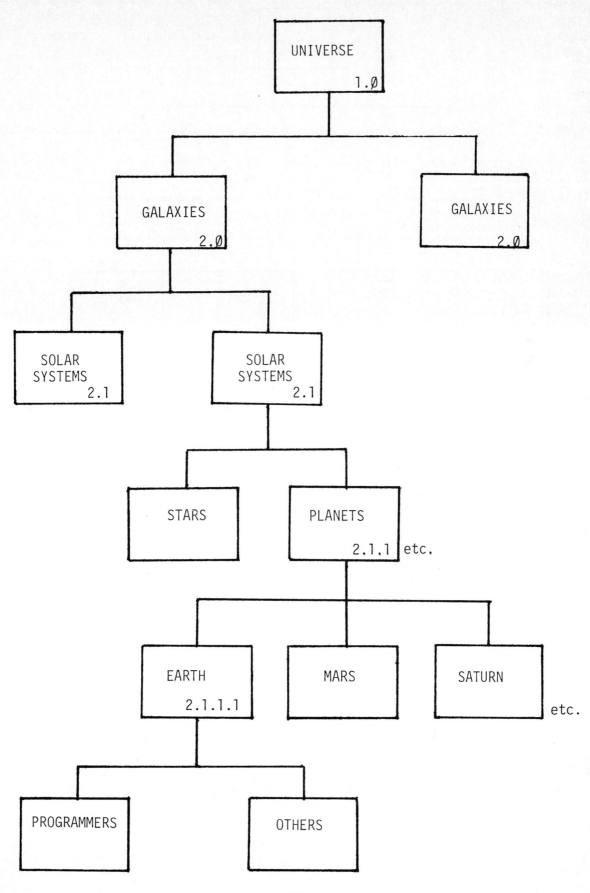

Geography:

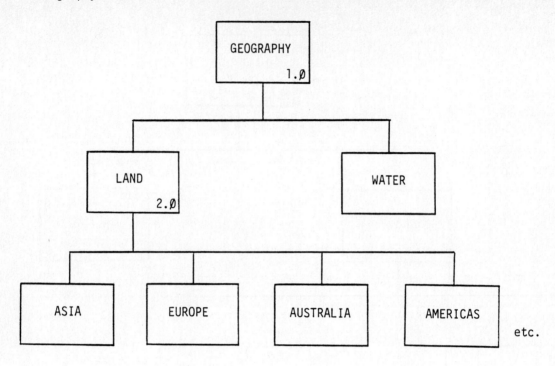

The U.S. Army, biological classifications, highway and road systems, and the nervous system are also complex systems that are hierarchical.

This is necessary in order to keep the number of relationships and logical connections to a minimum so we as humans can understand complex systems easier.

The systems just mentioned are pikers compared to some computer systems I have known when it comes to complexity. Programs and systems are innately complex, and we add to their complexity by not using a plan or a method in their development.

EXAMPLES

We will start with some simple specifications for our first example in designing a COBOL program using VTOCs.

Assume we want to find the mean of a set of integers being read in from a tape file (one integer per record).

Let's call our program find the mean.

```
┌──────────────┐
│  FIND THE    │
│   MEAN       │
│         1.Ø  │
└──────────────┘
```

The second level of most structured (VTOCed) programs looks the same.

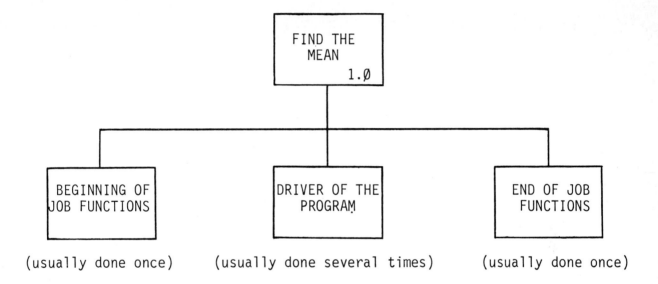

BEGINNING OF JOB FUNCTIONS (usually done once)   DRIVER OF THE PROGRAM (usually done several times)   END OF JOB FUNCTIONS (usually done once)

In our example we might have:

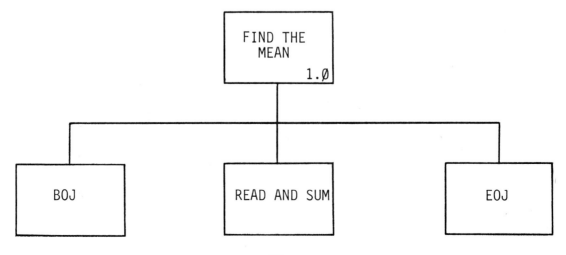

The <u>boj</u> function in most structured programs includes: opens; initialization of accumulators, counters, tables and switches; print header routines; and initial reads (to be discussed later).

In our program:

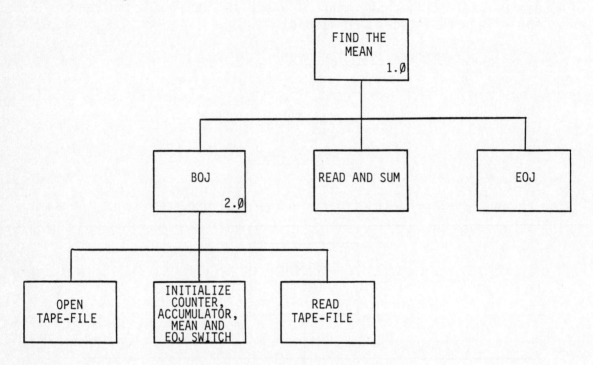

The "driver" function in most programs becomes a "loop" and includes all functions that have to be repeated in order to process the data.

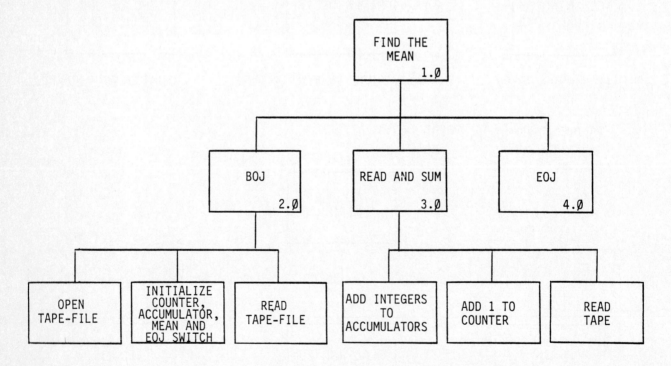

The _eoj_ contains final control totals, closes and stop run.

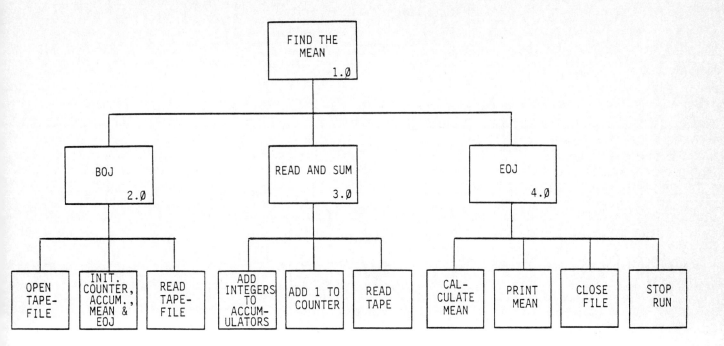

We now have a structural VTOC (design). In order to make it procedural we line up the modules left to right in the order we believe they need to be executed (which we have already done), and put conditions on them to control their execution.

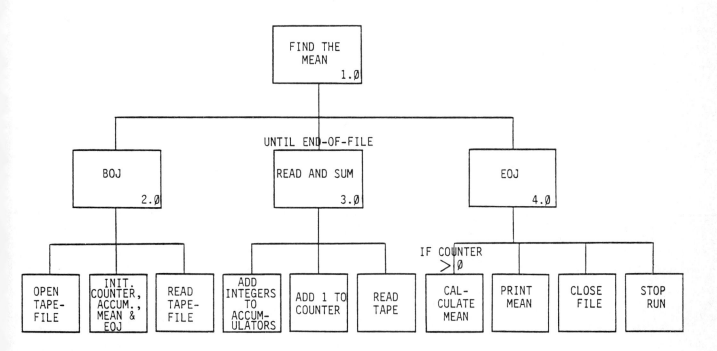

Our design is complete.

Notice the conditions are outside of the function and the bottom functions (which are not further decomposed) have no ID numbers in them.

In this example 1.∅ becomes the program name; 2.∅, 3.∅, and 4.∅ are paragraph names and the unnumbered functions become parts of paragraphs. In other words, in this example everything above the third level is a label.

We will find out how to code from VTOCs in the programming section. For the time being we will do one more program using VTOCs as our design tool.

Assume we want to design an edit and update program with the following specs.

We have two input files and one output. The master file is a sequential disk file sorted on the key called account-number. The transaction file is also a sequential disk file sorted on account-number. The updated master file will be a sequential disk also.

Both input files have been presorted and neither file has more than one record per account number.

An edit will be made on the transaction file involving three different fields. If an error is found on any of the three fields we will reject the entire transaction. (I.e., do not update the record unless all three fields pass the edit.)

An unmatched transaction record (no matching master record) will also be treated as an error (i.e., no addition of new records).

No print file will be defined; instead we will DISPLAY all edit and unmatched trans errors on the printer.

We will also DISPLAY a "before" and "after" on the fields we change. We therefore have three different types of print records: proof and edit, unmatched transaction account numbers, and a change record.

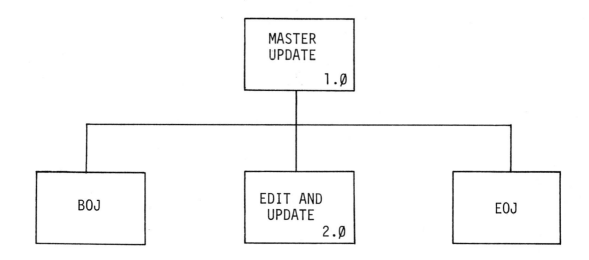

The first two levels of our design look like our previous example. Our program is called master update, and the boj routine contains our opens, initializations of switches, and two initial reads (master and transaction). Since we can picture in our minds the algorithm that is needed to implement boj, we will not decompose boj any further (applying the fourth "secondary principle of design").

The second function, edit and update, is probably too big a bite unless we break it down into smaller pieces, so we will number it (2.0), implying we want to decompose it further.

Eoj like boj is fairly small. In this case all we do is CLOSE files and STOP our run, therefore we will not decompose it.

In designing structured programs using VTOCs, there are certain patterns encountered so frequently that they almost become rules. Unfortunately, it's the exceptions that establish the rules so we will call them generalities (G's).

As we continue designing our program we will identify some of these G's.

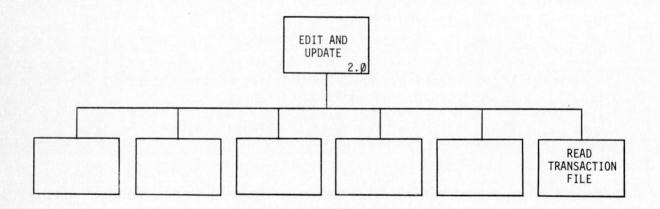

G-1. The only input files where you have to be careful when you read are the "driver files." (Driver files are those files that all other files react to.) In this example the transaction file is the driver file and the master file reacts to it.

G-2. Driver files should be read at the end of the level they are placed in.

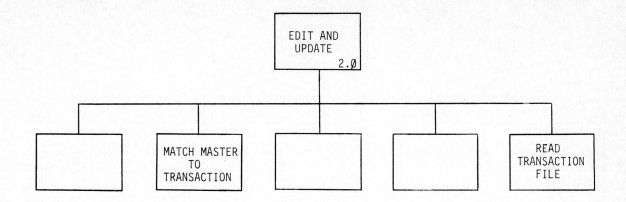

G-3. In update programs using sequential files, all "match" routines are implemented by writing and then reading the master file.

For example, assume our account numbers are the following:

Master-Acct	Transaction-Acct
1 - Read	6 - Read
3	8
5	10
6	11
7	

In <u>boj</u> the first record of each file is read.

Since we have sequential files we have to write out the account number 1 record before reading the second record account number 3 and so on until we get a match.

Master-Acct	Transaction-Acct
1st 2nd 1 - Read - Write	6 - Read
2nd 3rd 3 - Read - Write	8
3rd 4th 5 - Read - Write	10
4th 6 - Read	11

7

39

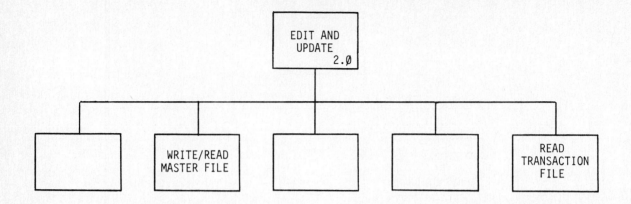

G-4.   In sequential file update programs, both master and transaction files should have initial reads.

G-5.   If you are within a loop (a function that is repeated), which edit and update is, it does not matter how you line up your functions if making it work is your only consideration.

We will line up the third level functions of our program in a certain order for the time being and then switch them around later to prove G-5.

G-6.   There should be only one function in your program that reads input files other than the initial read.

G-7.   There should be only one function in your program that writes output records from working-storage and only one for writing from the input buffer (FD).

G-6 and G-7 applied to our program say we can have no more read and write functions than we already have.   (We can read our master into working-storage and write from working-storage.)

Three other functions we will need for completing level three are an edit function, an error routine for mismatched transaction account numbers, and a change or update function (where we move the new fields into the master record).

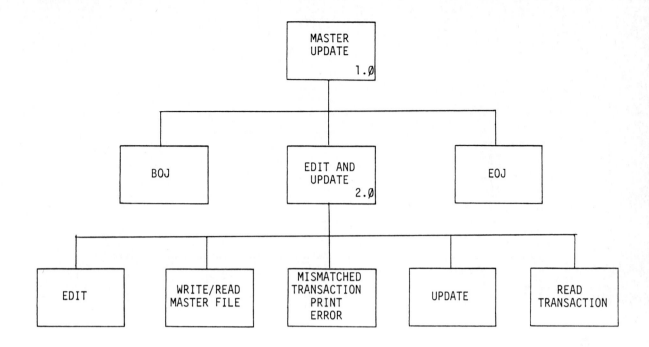

G-8. In sequential file processing, no special end-of-file processing
functions are needed if you design your program properly (structured) and
move HIGH-VALUES to the keys when the files go to AT END.

This will always work unless you have a key that has HIGH-VALUES as
a valid value.

The only additional process to consider before going to level four is
how can the edit function tell the update function if a bad record (failed
our edits) is passing through the level?

Yes, you're right, probably a nasty old switch has to be set in the
edit function and checked at the update function. Where should this edit
check switch be reset?

G-9. Switches that need resetting should be reset as the last process
in the level or the first.

We now decide if the function edit needs decomposing. This one's
marginal but since we have three fields to edit, let's do it.

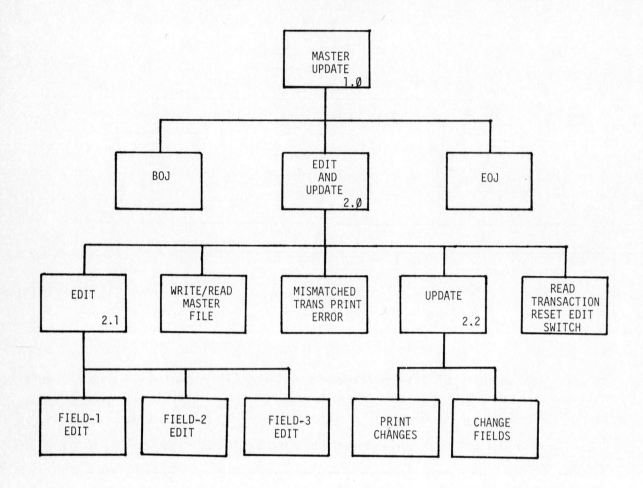

We could in turn decompose our three field edits into <u>display bad edit field on printer</u> and <u>set edit switch</u>, but that is probably too detailed. (Corollary: the programmer has to do something on his own.)

The second function, <u>write/read master file</u>, has only two functions in it, write and read, so we will not decompose it.

The third function is only displaying a print record so we will leave it alone.

The fourth function is changing the fields <u>and</u> printing out the before-and-after change report. Another marginal decision, but we will go ahead and break it down.

The last level three function is reading and resetting, with not much going on so we will leave it alone.

Our structural design (VTOC) is now complete.

Making it procedural requires the addition of conditions, since we have already logically lined up the functions within each level from left to right (e.g., boj, driver, eoj).

Going top-down left to right the top function is the program level, therefore the operator controls its execution.

Boj will always need execution if the program is executed, therefore no condition needs to be placed on boj.

The edit and update function becomes a loop and needs to be executed as long as we have master records or transaction records. Therefore we will define the eoj switch as including both end-of-transaction and end-of-master.

The eoj function needs no condition.

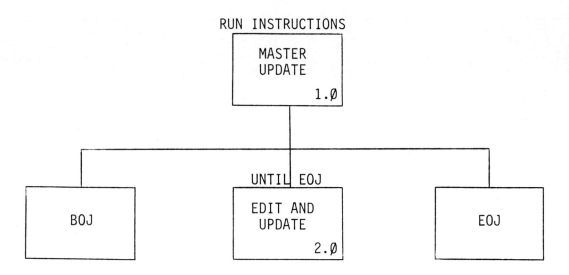

Third level conditions will include IF TRANSACTION-ACCOUNT ≠ HIGH-VALUES for the edit function and the read transaction function in the event the transaction file goes to AT END first and you have to go through the level to run out the master file.

G-1Ø. The only files you have to check to see if they are AT END is your driver files.

The master file will take care of itself if you move HIGH-VALUES to the account numbers when the AT END condition is met and you apply G-6.

The condition that controls our write/read master will be "UNTIL M-ACCT ≥ T-ACCT."

The mismatched trans print error needs an "IF M >T." The update needs at least two conditions: "IF M = T" and "IF EDIT-OK."

All of the functions in the fourth level are unconditionally executed.

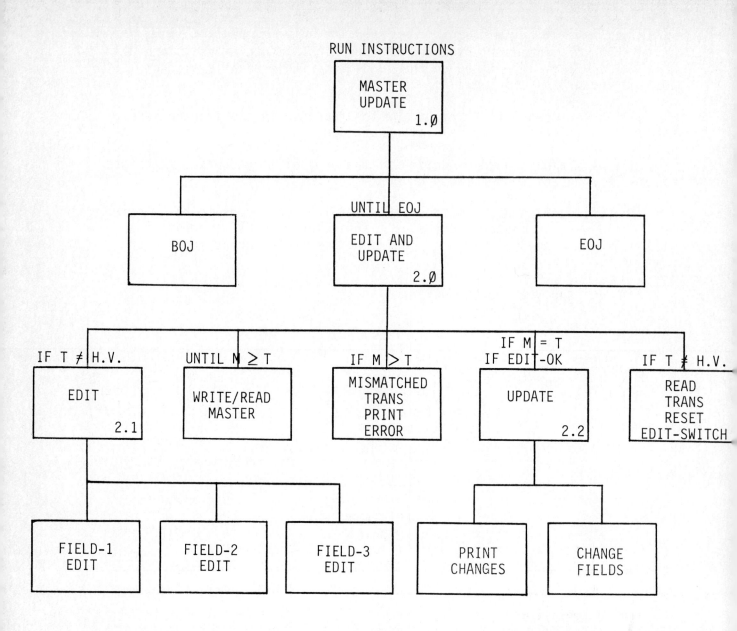

RUN INSTRUCTIONS

Notice once again that the conditions that control the execution of the functions are outside of the module, that bottom functions are numberless, that each function having a number in it becomes a paragraph in the COBOL program, and all functions under it become part of that paragraph.

When the VTOC is complete the logic should be thoroughly tested. Logic errors should be caught at the design stage, not at the coding stage. In a pictorial VTOC it is easier to catch bugs than in a source-listing narrative.

Which of the following methods are ways to "catch bugs"?

A)   Sleep in the grass.
B)   Don't wash your hair.
C)   Be a dog.
D)   Walk through the logic using test data.

Answer: all of the above, but we will only talk about "D."

Here are some test transactions.

Master-Acct-#s	Trans-Acct-#s	Edit	Output Master
4	5	Good	
5	7	No Good	
7	8	No Good	
9	10	Good	
10	11	Good	
11	12	Good	

The operator executes <u>master update</u>. (Make sure your run instructions are accurate.)

<u>Boj</u> executes reading the first record on each file.

Master	Trans
4 - Read	5 - Read

The <u>edit and update</u> executes since we are not at <u>eoj</u>.

The <u>edit</u> function executes, telling us we have a good record edit-wise.

The until $M \geq T$ checks the account numbers and determines that the <u>write/read master</u> should be executed since $4 < 5$.

Master	Trans	Edit	Output Master
4 - Read-Write	5 - Read	Good	4
5 - Read			

Since $M \not> T$, <u>mismatched trans</u> is not executed.

Since $M = T$ and "Edit is good", <u>update</u> is executed and the changes are made and printed.

Another trans record is read and we repeat the levels since <u>eoj</u> is still false.

Master	Trans	Edit	Output Master
4 - Read-Write	5 - Read	Good	4
5 - Read	7 - Read	No Good	

This time, though, the edit is no good, so the edit messages are
displayed, indicating which fields are in error. The write/read master
writes out the 5 record (which we updated the last time through the record),
and the master record 7 is read. Since 7 on the trans is equal to 7 on the
master, the write/read master does not execute again. (Remember the PERFORM
UNTIL always checks the condition first before executing the process.)

We now have:

Master	Trans	Edit	Output Master
4 - Read-Write	5 - Read	Good	4
5 - Read-Write	7 - Read	No Good	5
7 - Read			

We do not execute the next two functions. Since M $\neq$ T and edit is
no good, we end up reading another transaction (account number 8), and
repeating the level.

Master	Trans	Edit	Output Master
4 - Read-Write	5 - Read	Good	4
5 - Read-Write	7 - Read	No Good	5
7 - Read-Write	8 - Read	No Good	7
9 - Read			

This time the edit is no good, the 7 Master Record is written to
Output Master, the 9 Master Record is read, the mismatched trans routine
is executed, indicating that the 8 trans record does not exist on the
master, and another transaction record is read (account number 10).

Master	Trans	Edit	Output Master
4 - Read-Write	5 - Read	Good	4
5 - Read-Write	7 - Read	No Good	5
7 - Read-Write	8 - Read	No Good	7
9 - Read	10 - Read	Good	

The next time through the level yields:

Master	Trans	Edit	Output Master
4 - Read-Write	5	Good	4
5 - Read-Write	7	No Good	5
7 - Read-Write	8	No Good	7
9 - Read-Write	10	Good	9
10 - Read-Write	11	Good	10
11 - Read			

The next iteration gives us:

Master	Trans	Edit	Output Master
4 - Read-Write	5	Good	4
5 - Read-Write	7	No Good	5
7 - Read-Write	8	No Good	7
9 - Read-Write	10	Good	9
10 - Read-Write	11	Good	10
11 - Read-Write	12	Good	11
High Values			

Notice that the master is forced to AT END, moving HIGH-VALUES to the master account number. The 12 record of the transaction file is printed out as an error since HIGH-VALUES > 12, and then the trans file is forced to AT END, terminating the job since EOJ = END-OF-MASTER + END-OF-TRANS.

So far, the logic works. One other test you should always try is alternating the file which runs out first. Giving the master file a higher account number, say 14, your end processing would look like this:

Master	Trans	Edit	Output Master
11 - Read-Write	High-Values	Good	11
14 - Read			

Now when you hit the <u>write/read master</u> function, the master account number turns to HIGH-VALUES after writing out the 14 record, and both account numbers are HIGH-VALUE. But we obviously have a problem because M = T and EDIT IS OKAY, forcing us to do the <u>update</u> function when we do not have any records.

G-11. If the structural VTOC is complete (includes all functions necessary to do the job), any bug that occurs in a loop can be fixed by adding a condition.

In our case, adding the condition IF T ≠ HIGH-VALUES above the <u>update</u> function will correct the bug.

Another way of stating G-11 is to say as long as you're in a loop it does not matter how you line up your functions if you have included all of them.

For example, if our third level had been completely reversed, let's say the <u>read transaction</u> function came first instead of last, we still could have made it work. All we would have had to do was put another switch on it, "IF NOT FIRST TIME," which would have allowed us to skip it the first time through.

G-12. Any logical arrangement of functions within a loop can be forced to work by putting more conditions on them to control their execution.

G-13. If you see a program that has an extreme number of conditions that control execution of the processes, the processes could have been reordered and sequenced better to cut down the number of execution controlling conditions (i.e., fewer switches).

Before leaving this section on VTOCs, one more observation should be made. Flowcharts ≠ VTOCs. Traditionally (at least the way I was taught), you first drew a flowchart and then coded from it. I could always think in COBOL better than I could in flowcharts, so I would write the program and draw the flowchart from the code, convincing my supervisor that the flowchart came first. But in structured COBOL, flowcharts are (almost) worthless.

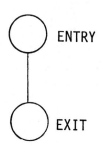

Assume the above diagram represents a COBOL program. The entry is the beginning of the program; the exit is the STOP RUN.

The simplest program you could write would be one in which you execute one instruction after the other until you come to the exit. There would only be one way through the program.

Look what happens by adding one branch. (In COBOL, IF COND-A GO TO X.)

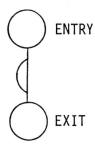

Now there are two ways through the program.

ENTRY

EXIT

Adding another branch gives you four ways that the logic can flow through the program.

Three branches yield a combination of 8 possible logic flows.

Possible ways through Program = 2^N where N is the number of conditional branches.

If you only had 40 conditional branches in a program (I've seen them with 100s), you would have to test a different way through the program every second in order to have all the possible logic flows tested in 17,432 years.

That's why a program will run for 11 years, and then one night at 2 a.m. in the morning you will get a call because it bombed. It found a different way through the program.

The point is this: PROCESSES DO NOT MAKE PROGRAMS COMPLEX. IT IS THE FLOW OF THE LOGIC. The functions executed are not the complicating factors in programs; it is how you get to the process to execute it.

That is how flowcharts differ from VTOCs. Flowcharts define the functions and then flow around executing them at random. VTOCs define the functions and execute them one after the other, TOP-DOWN, until the EXIT is reached. (A VTOC is read top-down, left to right.)

One more example is shown to illustrate this.

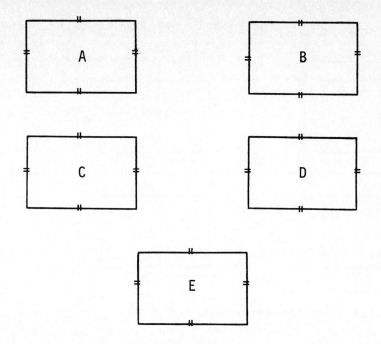

Assume these five boxes represent buildings on a college campus. Each building has a door on each side. Our job is to trace a student's flow through the buildings throughout the day. Designing by flowcharts we would do it this way.

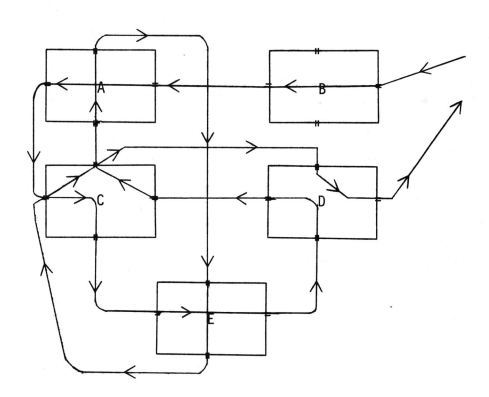

Using VTOCs to design the same system, you would have the following.

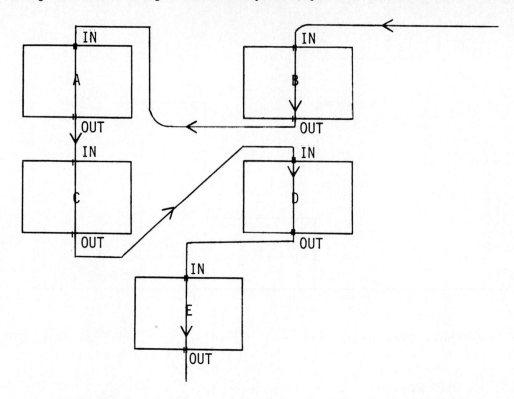

Notice the same buildings are being used, except there are only two doors in each building, and each door is an "in" or an "out" door.

Tracing the student through the buildings there soon comes a time when we need to get to a building we have already been through. Since we are not flowcharting, we can not just "go to" the building. Do we have any other options? We could go back to the top, retracing our steps until we arrived at the building we wanted, but that seems to be the long way around.

The best way to keep it top-down is to:

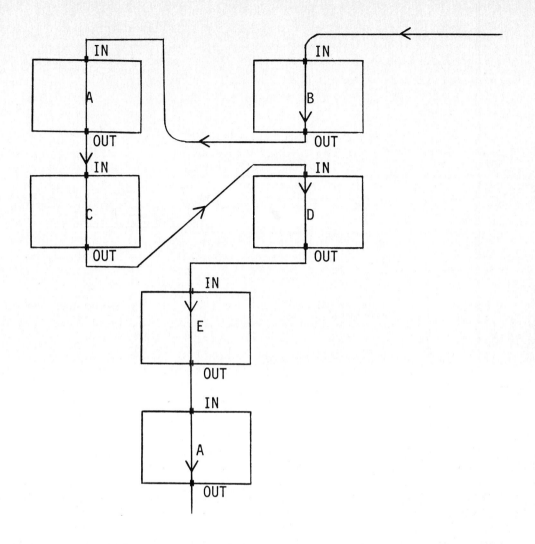

That's right, we have to build building A again so we can keep our logic flowing top-down, executing one instruction after the other. Admittedly, if this was a college campus there would be quite a waste of resources erecting extra buildings on campus to keep the student's flow top-down, but in a COBOL program it is quite simple; you build the paragraph only once and when you need it, you perform it. That is how you keep your flow top-down.

The primary purpose, therefore, of structured design/programming is to keep the programs easy to understand and as simple as possible. Why this is necessary can be illustrated with the following graph.

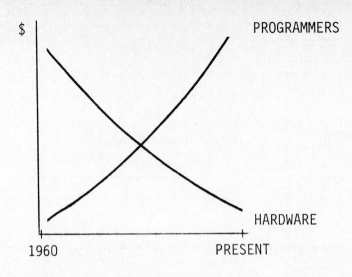

In the early days of computer application, the hardware was very expensive and there was very little of it. Therefore, programmers spent a good part of their time conserving the scarce computer resource, making it fit in limited capacity machines with limited cycle speed. We tended not to worry about writing easily understood code, as long as it worked, who cared? Times have changed. Hardware is getting cheaper, people are becoming more expensive; now in order to hold down costs you have to hold down the people costs. Since over 50% of the cost of a system over its lifetime is spent in maintaining it, you have to hold down maintenance costs to hold down expenditures. Since maintenance is people intensive (not hardware intensive), you have to be able to develop easily understood systems and programs that take a minimum of people involvement to maintain them. Whereas in days gone by the emphasis was on "make it work," today it is K.I.S.S.

I have been acquainted with systems and programs that took literally weeks trying to understand so that a relatively minor change could be made (and even then you were generally wrong and it took several changes to make it work).

Therefore, structured programming is an attempt to (make programs simple so they can be easily understood so they can be easily maintained so you can) save dollars. If it doesn't do it, throw it out!

Designing with VTOCs, in my opinion, is using the best structured tool available. Nevertheless, there are two areas in which VTOCs are lacking at the program level. The first of these is the obvious deficiency of not allowing a place to define your input and output, data bases, files, records, fields or characters. The second one is the inability to expand the bottom modules (the working code) to explain complex or nonstandard code since each module is a function name and not the working code per se. By the way, if needed, narrative can be used with upper level modules (label modules) to define and support the design, since many functions might be used that are unclear as to what they include or what the original designer had in mind.

When defining the bottom modules, since they resolve themselves into the actual code in a program, the COBOL code itself in most cases can serve as the documentation and needs no further narrative. The exception to this again is the cases where the program designer needs to elaborate on some unusual code to communicate more clearly with the coder. In these cases HIPOs in conjunction with PSEUDO-CODE can be used to document and clarify the code.

As with VTOCs, doing a HIPO will probably accomplish more than talking about them; hence our first example.

HIPOs should be used in conjunction with your system/program VTOC. In the section on VTOCs we developed the following program.

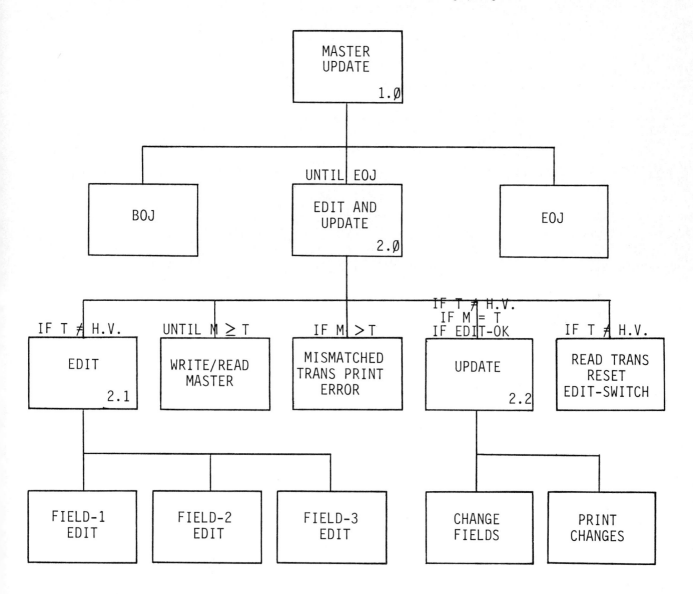

HIPOs can represent systems, subsystems, programs or paragraphs in programs. In other words, there can be one HIPO per function of a VTOC for all functions of a VTOC that are decomposed. (You do not create separate HIPOs for the bottom functions.)

In our program VTOC, in order to completely HIPO it we would need four HIPOs. One for 1.0, 2.0, 2.1 and 2.2 since those are the only modules which have other functions under them.

SYSTEM NAME   NAME-OF-SYSTEM
SUBSYSTEM NAME   NAME-OF-SUBSYSTEM
PROGRAM NAME   MASTER UPDATE
FUNCTION NAME   MASTER UPDATE
FUNCTION I.D. NUMBER   1.0

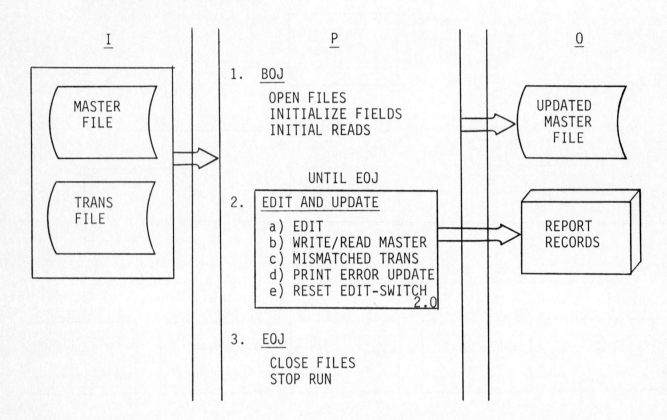

The master update HIPO is a program HIPO; it represents the overall view of our program. HIPOs consist of three columns: Input (I), Process (P), and Output (O). The process column is the easiest to complete since the VTOC itself defines all the processes for us. The three processes boj, edit and update, and eoj are lined up in order in the process column. Boj and eoj functions on the HIPO are not boxed and have no function ID number. Since edit and update is decomposed, you box it, number it, and indicate the functions within it (a, b, c, d, e). Notice that one HIPO can illustrate three levels of a VTOC.

Next, identify your input and output. We have two input files, one output file, and three types of output print records.

To complete the HIPO, draw arrows from the input to process and process to output column, indicating what processes use which files and records, and what processes are creating the output files and records.

Our arrows indicate that all three functions are doing input operations on both master and trans file (open, read, close). All three functions also create the updated master (open, write, close), but the edit and update is the only function creating the print reports since we do not have a print file. (We are displaying our print records.)

The next HIPO (top-down, left to right) would be <u>edit and update</u>, 2.0.

<u>PROGRAM NAME</u>   MASTER UPDATE
<u>FUNCTION NAME</u>   EDIT AND UPDATE
<u>FUNCTION ID NUMBER</u>   2.0

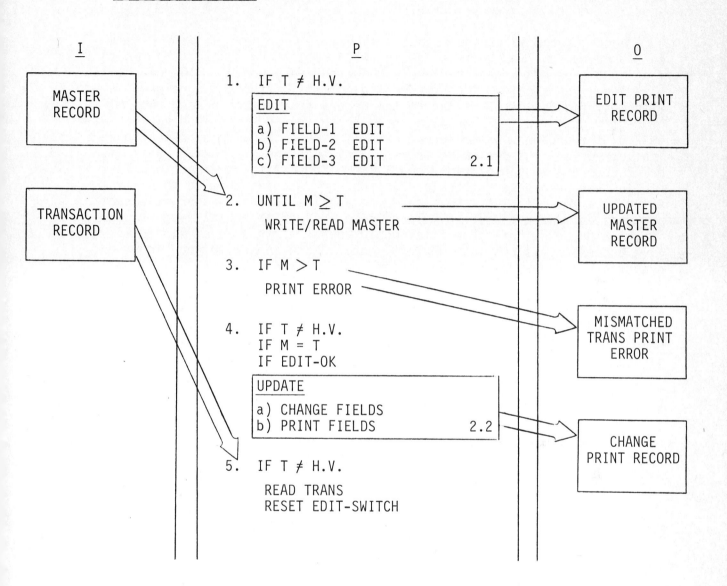

Please notice the following HIPO format rules.

On 1.0 the highest data structure being processed was a file, therefore the file symbol was used for the master and transaction data.

In 2.0 the highest data structures being processed are records, therefore record symbols are used.

This shows that 1.0 handled all of the file processing (opens and closes), and by the time you arrive at the second level no files are in view.

Then, notice that you draw the arrows only if an actual I/O operation is taking place (OPEN, CLOSE, READ, WRITE, ACCEPT, DISPLAY, RETURN, RELEASE, REWRITE, SEEK, START, DELETE, INITIATE, GENERATE, TERMINATE, EXHIBIT). The edit function uses fields on the transaction record but no arrow is drawn to indicate this, only where the READ is taking place is one used. This helps to keep your HIPO neat.

Next, as the input and output drop out of your design, define them. In 2.0 every function that is reading your master and transaction record is down to the pseudo-code (they are not further decomposed). Therefore, at this level you should define the record formats of these two records (lengths, fields, etc.). Placing the record description behind this HIPO or referring to an I/O book with the description in it is acceptable. Also on 2.0, the updated master record and mismatched trans print report have "fallen" out of the design so the same thing applies to them. The edit print record and change print record are being created by functions that are further decomposed, therefore you do not describe them at this level. Going up a level to 1.0, the same thing applies to your master, transaction, and updated master files. All three descriptions (blocking factors, label information, etc.) of these files would appear at this level since all your file processing is complete on level one. Again, describe your input and output as it drops out of your design.

The fourth format rule is watch how your arrows are drawn. An arrow that stops at the edge of the process or output column indicates that everything in the column is included, whereas an arrow that crosses the column boundary is pointing to a particular function or output. This applies not only to where an arrow ends, but also to where it starts.

The next HIPO is 2.1.

PROGRAM NAME   MASTER UPDATE
FUNCTION NAME   EDIT
FUNCTION ID NUMBER   2.1

I   P   O

    1. IF FIELD-1 BAD
            SET EDIT-SWITCH
            PRINT EDIT-RECORD

                                                          EDIT
                                                          PRINT
                                                          RECORD

    2. IF FIELD-2 BAD
            SET EDIT-SWITCH
            PRINT EDIT-RECORD

    3. IF FIELD-3 BAD
            SET EDIT-SWITCH
            PRINT EDIT-RECORD

All three functions are pseudo-coded, and the edit print record is described.

The last HIPO is 2.2.

PROGRAM NAME   MASTER UPDATE
FUNCTION NAME   UPDATE
FUNCTION ID NUMBER   2.2.

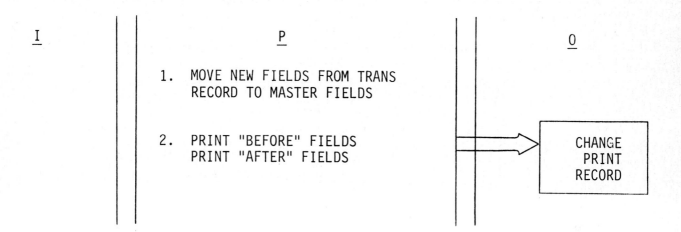

I

P

O

1.   MOVE NEW FIELDS FROM TRANS
     RECORD TO MASTER FIELDS

2.   PRINT "BEFORE" FIELDS
     PRINT "AFTER" FIELDS

CHANGE
PRINT
RECORD

Again, all functions are pseudo-coded, and the print record is described.

Summarizing the section on HIPOs, remember their main contribution is to allow you to define your input and output and/or describe in pseudo-code unusual or complex code.

The number of functions HIPOed in your design depends on how much precode documentation and design effort you want. In a COBOL environment sometimes it becomes overkill to HIPO every function in a program VTOC since COBOL is a self documenting language, in which case the code itself is sufficient to document and explain the module.

3.0 PROGRAMMING

CONCEPTS AND METHODOLOGY

There are two ways you can write a structured COBOL program.

1) Develop a VTOC and/or HIPO (or combination thereof), and code directly from the VTOC and/or HIPO (or combination thereof).

2) Throw out VTOCs and HIPOs and follow the Six Rules of Structured COBOL Programming.

Method one and method two will yield the same final results, but method one is probably the superior method for reasons to be discussed later.

Method two is nothing more than following rules that make your program look like a VTOC. Stated differently, method two will produce results that make it appear as if you designed your program first using VTOCs/HIPOs.

In applying method one, basically only two techniques have to be learned. If the function is decomposed you perform it, or if the function is executed more than once in the program you perform it, otherwise you in-line expand it. In other words, the PERFORM in COBOL is used to implement the levels of a VTOC.

Referring back to our Master Update Program, coding from the VTOC, the first level of the program would become:

```
          ***** LEVEL A *****
          A-010-MASTER-UPDATE-10.
                 ⎧ OPEN----
                 ⎪ MOVE----
          BOJ  ⎨ MOVE----
                 ⎪ PERFORM C-010-READ-MASTER
                 ⎩ PERFORM C-020-READ-TRANSACTION
          EDIT AND ⎰ PERFORM B-010-EDIT-UPDATE
            UPDATE ⎱      UNTIL EOJ
                 ⎰ CLOSE----
          EOJ ⎱ STOP RUN
                   .
```

The first paragraph name in level A is also the program name, since master-update contains the entire program.

Boj is "in-line expanded" (as opposed to performed), since it is not decomposed. There you open and initialize your fields in level A. The two perform statements in the boj function are the result of encountering two functions that are executed more than once in the program. These common routines, C-010-READ-MASTER and C-020-READ-TRANSACTION are placed in the C level of the program since the B level is the lowest level that executes them.

Since the edit-and-update function is decomposed, you perform it, pushing it down to level B.

62

A performed paragraph is placed one level lower than the lowest level that performs it.

The eoj function is all in-line expanded since it is not decomposed and there are no common routines.

Obviously, coding from the VTOC requires a little imagination since boj and eoj were not detailed on the VTOC.

Looking at the HIPO 1.0 instead of the VTOC, it is obvious that programming from either one would yield the same results. The HIPO has more detail (pseudo-code), and you would perform any function on a HIPO that is boxed. But since there is a one-to-one correspondence between VTOC and HIPO, either design tool can be directly coded into COBOL.

There are two distinct advantages in using method one over method two (designing by VTOCing, as opposed to designing "on the fly") in developing programs. The first one concerns documentation. If VTOCs and HIPOs are used, they serve not only as a program design tool, but also may be retained and used as documentation. The best documentation for systems and programs is the documentation derived while analyzing, designing, coding, and implementing the systems and programs; not something that is tacked on as an afterthought. The "document it after you write it" philosophy tends to produce unuseful documentation if it ever gets documented. This of course violates one of the basic laws of programming, which states: "The Quantity of Program Documentation is inversely related to the Quality of the Program: QPD = 1/QP."

The second advantage deals with debugging the code. First, a pictorial representation of a program (VTOC) tends to be easier to catch bugs with than a narrative representation (the actual code). Second, you do not have to rewrite and undo bad code when you find the bug. Nevertheless, we will spend the next few pages developing the Six Rules of Structured COBOL Programming (method two).

Rule one: Any program can be written in COBOL using only three logic structures.

The problem with logic structures is that programmers tend to think in a language (like COBOL) rather than logic structures. A logic structure is a basic structure or form in which logic may be expressed and is applicable to any language.

The three logic structures we are primarily interested in are called the sequential logic structure, the if-else logic structure, and the iterative logic structure.

The sequential structure is simply executing one instruction after the other, which COBOL handles quite nicely.

```
MOVE----
ADD----
COMPUTE----
PERFORM----
WRITE----

.
```

The IF-ELSE is also easily implemented in COBOL:

```
IF CONDITION A
    DO B
ELSE
    DO C
.
```

The iterative or "loop" logic structure consists of two structures: the do while and the do until. Here is where you have to throw 90% of the textbooks out the window due to the wrong definitions given these two.

The do while says do something (a process), while the condition is true and the do until says do something until it is true.

In COBOL: PERFORM PARAGRAPH-A
                 UNTIL CONDITION IS NOT TRUE

is the do while, and

            PERFORM PARAGRAPH-A
                UNTIL CONDITION IS TRUE

is the do until.

In flowchart symbols:

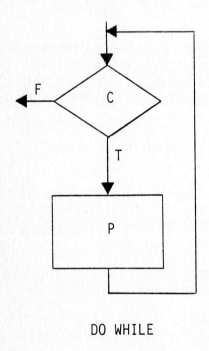

DO WHILE

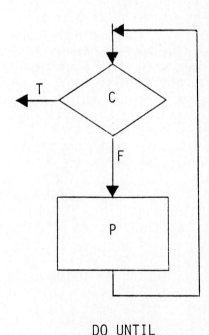

DO UNTIL

Most textbooks insist that the do while logic structure is one where the condition is checked first, and then the process is executed, and the do until is where the process is executed first and then the condition is checked.

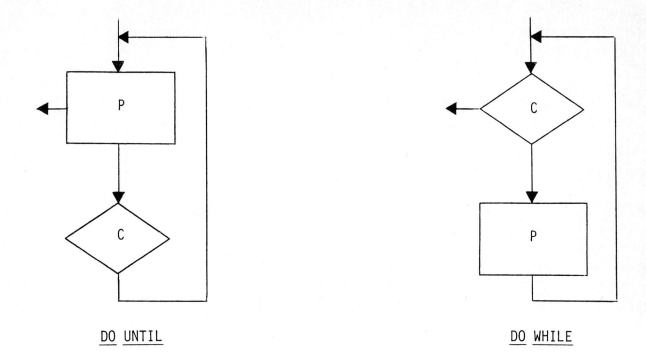

DO UNTIL   DO WHILE

I have yet to determine what these interpretations have to do with the do while and do until logic structures.

To keep them straight in your mind, simply think of them as their name implies; do while something is true, and do until something is true.

Rule two: Every module (process, function or box) can have only one exit and one entry.

It's apparent from a VTOC that you cannot have more than one way in or out of a function.

65

EVERY MODULE
CAN HAVE ONLY
ONE EXIT AND
ONE ENTRY

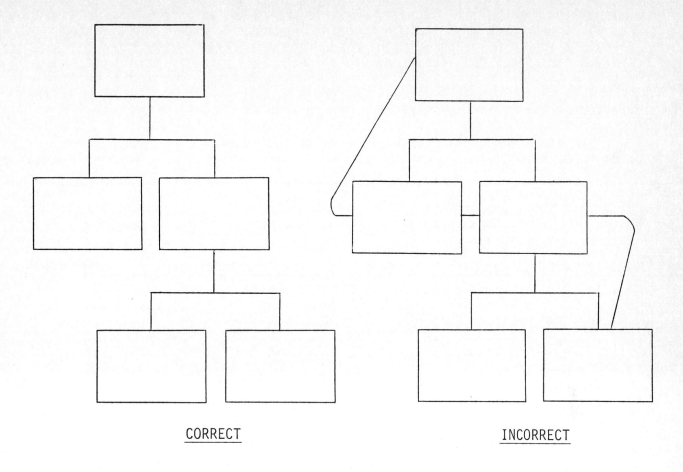

CORRECT   INCORRECT

    The application of this rule has some interesting effects. It would
mean a system or subsystem can have only one way in and one way out
(computer operators would love you). Programs can have only one way in and
one way out (only one STOPRUN).

    Paragraphs can only have one entry and one exit. This eliminates the
perform through verb and section names.

              INCORRECT   CORRECT
           PERFORM A THRU C   PERFORM A
                                                         PERFORM B
                                                         PERFORM C

    A.

    B.

    C.

    Using the PERFORM THRU allows a module to have more than one entry
and/or exit, because another statement in your program could be executing
B only (PERFORM B). Incidentally, PERFORM THRUs are hard to maintain due
to the intermediate paragraph names (in our case B) not appearing in your
cross-reference.

67

Sections are also no-no's, since that would be a sneaky way of doing a PERFORM THRU. Of course, in the case where the COBOL snytax demands a section name (the SORT verb) they are allowed.

Rule three: Initial reads. This rule to which we have alluded to in the previous sections is necessary in order to keep structured code clean.

Structured programs eventually (due to the adherence to rules) start looking alike.

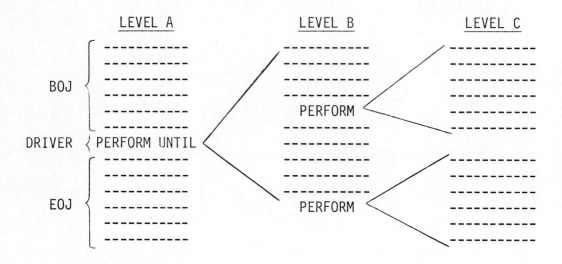

Level A generally has your beginning of job routines, a driver that pushes you down a level, and an end-of-job routine. Level B in turn has some modules in-line-expanded and some performed, which in turn shoves you down another level, and so on.

G-14. A program with more than seven or eight levels is too large and should be broken into two or more programs. (I.e., the program was defined too high up on the VTOC.)

Using an example to illustrate the Initial Read rule, assume we have a program that reads a sequential file record, alters several fields on the record, and writes it out to a sequential output file. If initial reads had not been used then the first instruction in level B would have to be a READ.

<u>LEVEL B</u>

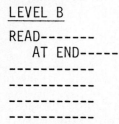

```
READ-------
    AT END-----
    -----------
    -----------
    -----------
    -----------
```

The problem with this code is when the file goes to end, we have to either A) set a switch, B) use a branch, or C) introduce another exit.

A) <u>LEVEL B</u>

```
READ-------
    AT END MOVE 'Y' TO EOJ-SW
.
IF NOT EOJ
        ----------
        ----------
        ----------
.
IF NOT EOJ
        ----------
        ----------
        ----------
.
```

B) <u>LEVEL B</u>

```
READ-------
    AT END GO TO EXIT
.
    ----------
    ----------
    ----------
    ----------
EXIT.
```

C) <u>LEVEL B</u>

```
READ-------
    AT END STOP RUN
.
    ----------
    ----------
    ----------
```

All the previous examples either violate one of our six rules or introduce sloppy code.

Using the initial read, we would end up with:

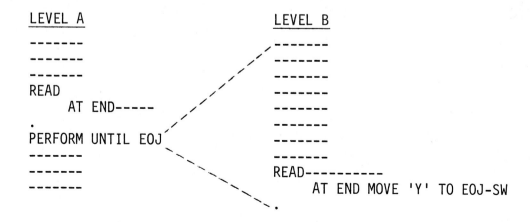

<u>LEVEL A</u>

```
-------
-------
-------
READ
    AT END-----
.
PERFORM UNTIL EOJ
-------
-------
-------
```

<u>LEVEL B</u>

```
-------
-------
-------
-------
-------
-------
-------
-------
READ----------
    AT END MOVE 'Y' TO EOJ-SW
.
```

There has probably been more written about Rule Four than all other structured rules combined.

Rule four: No go-tos. First of all, "Let me make this perfectly clear...," you can write sloppy, hard to understand COBOL programs and never use a GO TO.

Leaving out go-tos does not insure that you are writing an easily understood program or that it is structured.

The reason this is so is because the "no go-to" rule is a result, not a cause.

If a book falls on the floor creating a loud noise, the noise did not cause the book to fall; it was only a result of its falling. The same goes for go-tos. If you design a well-structured program, the end result will be go-to-less code. The important issue is good design, not leaving out go-tos.

Rule five. In-line expand all code unless the code in question is large, complex, or repetitive.

When designing a program using VTOCs, it has already been determined if a module should be performed (if it's decomposed or common), or if it should be in-line expanded. If you are following the six rules to develop your program, that decision has to be made as you code.

If the code in question is large (causing a paragraph to exceed one page on the source listing), break it up into two or more paragraphs and perform them.

If the code in question is complex, pull it out and make a separate paragraph of it. For instance, if you were in a payroll program and you wanted to calculate FICA you might not want to stick that computation in the middle of a paragraph that is doing something else. If for no other reason than for documentation purposes, it probably should be performed as a separate paragraph.

If the code in question is repetitive (executed from more than one place in the program), again you put it in a separate paragraph one level lower than the last level that executes it, and perform it.

Rule six: Use structured periods. I would guess that more time is spent debugging COBOL programs due to missing or misplaced periods than any other single COBOL synedoche with the possible exception of REPORT WRITER.

The structured period rule says, "Get those little rascals under control."

```
PARAGRAPH-A.
     OPEN INPUT FILE NAME
     MOVE ZERO TO DATA-NAME-1
                  DATA-NAME-2
                  DATA-NAME-3
     PERFORM READ-FILE
     PERFORM PROCESS-FILE
             UNTIL EOF
     IF ERR-SWITCH-ON
        DISPLAY MESSAGE
     .
     CLOSE FILE
     STOP RUN
     .
```

The structured period applies only to the algorithm in the procedure division.

1) Only use periods where the logic demands it and to terminate paragraphs.

2) Put the period in column 12 on a line by itself.

A guarantee: If the only thing you apply from this booklet is the structured period, your boss will still fall down and call you blessed.

Notice in our example we could have used several periods to terminate the statements, but the logic is unaltered by omitting them. The only two periods used were for terminating a conditional (IF ELSE) and terminating the paragraph.

By the way, the following are some COBOL conditionals to watch out for:

```
IF
ON
AT END
AT END-OF-PAGE
INVALID KEY
WHEN
CHANGED
ON SIZE ERROR

.
```

We now have six rules that, if adhered to, will result in a COBOL program that will look as if it had been VTOCed.

To establish these rules we have three exceptions.

Generally, exceptions occur due to the weakness of the language, not the weakness of the rules.

Rule one exception: A fourth logic structure called the case logic structure is used in many COBOL environments.

THE STRUCTURED PERIOD ADWARD

In COBOL the case logic structure is implemented by the GO TO DEPENDING ON.

If, for instance, you have an edit program that edits one hundred different transaction record types (1-100), you would need one hundred IF statements to determine which edit routine to execute.

Using the GO TO DEPENDING ON greatly simplifies the logic but violates rule one by adding a new logic structure, and violates rule four by adding numerous GO-TOs.

However, the entire structure is still structured (one entry/one exit).

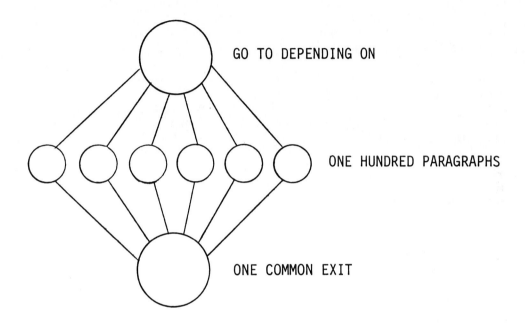

GO TO DEPENDING ON

ONE HUNDRED PARAGRAPHS

ONE COMMON EXIT

Rule four exception: In addition to using GO-TOs in the case logic structure, some COBOL environments also use intra-modular go-tos.

There are three types of branches in a COBOL program.

1) Intra-statement branch. Conditionals in COBOL are intra-statement branches.

```
IF COND-A
    DO PROCESS-B
ELSE
    NEXT SENTENCE
.
```

They branch to the period.

Of course, these are <u>always</u> allowed in structured code.

2) Intra-modular branch. These are branches that take you to the end (EXIT) of the paragraph or module.

```
PARAGRAPH-A
     IF COND-A
         GO TO PARA-A-EXIT
     .
     MOVE----
     ADD----
     COMPUTE----
     .
PARA-A-EXIT.
```

These are <u>sometimes allowed</u>, depending on your shop standards. I
personally do not like them. They allow a programmer to be less diligent
in his/her design of modules. I have observed over many years of writing
COBOL that structured code tends to be "tighter," using fewer lines of
code than nonstructured code, even within the paragraphs.

3) Inter-modular branch. These are branches that take you from one
module to another.

```
PARAGRAPH-A
     IF COND-A
         GO TO PARAGRAPH-C
     .
PARAGRAPH-B.
     ----------
     ----------
PARAGRAPH-C.
     ----------
     ----------
```

These, of course, are never allowed.

Rule five exception: Paragraphs that have been set up to implement
the iterative logic structures (PERFORM UNTIL) can be left on the same
level in which they are performed.

It would be nice if COBOL had END statements.

```
IF COND-A                    or          READ FILE-NAME
    DO PROCESS B                              AT END
END-IF                                   END-READ
```

or best of all,

```
PERFORM UNTIL EOJ
     ADD-----
     MOVE-----
     COMPUTE-----
     PERFORM-----
END-PERFORM
```

74

This would allow you to in-line expand the do while and do until logic structures.

Unfortunately, we do not have END-PERFORMS. Therefore, in order to implement the iterative logic structure in COBOL, you have to put the code in a paragraph and then PERFORM UNTIL. Therefore, we are forced to perform a module that is not large, complex, or repetitive (executed from more than one place in the program), which violates rule five.

If the only purpose in setting up a new paragraph is to implement the iterative logic structure, you may leave the performed paragraph on the same level it is performed. Of course, if the logic in the paragraph is large, complex, or repetitive, then it should be dropped a level.

```
      ***** LEVEL A *****

         ----------
         ----------
         PERFORM PARAGRAPH-A
             UNTIL EOJ
         ----------
         ----------
         ----------
         ----------
      PARAGRAPH-A.
         --SMALL, NONCOMPLEX, OR NONREPETITIVE CODE--


      ***** LEVEL A *****

         ----------
         ----------
         PERFORM PARAGRAPH-A
             UNTIL EOJ
         ----------
         ----------
         ----------


      ***** LEVEL B *****

      PARAGRAPH-A
         --LARGE, COMPLEX, OR REPETITIVE CODE--
```

This concludes our six rules and three exceptions.

EXAMPLES

To illustrate their application, we will walk through a simple example.

Two input sequential files, one output sequential file: Record formats are identical on all three files with the key in the first ten bytes. Our job, should we choose to accept it, is to create the output file from records on the input files that have matching keys. If a record on one input file has the same key as one on the second input file, write them both out to the output file. We can assume both input files have been sorted on the key and we do not have duplicate keys on either input file. We, of course, will have duplicate keys on the output file. We will also DISPLAY the total number of records written to the output file on the printer.

```
 1    ***** LEVEL A *****
 2      A-Ø1Ø-CREATE-FILE.
 3          OPEN INPUT FILE-1
 4                      FILE-2
 5               OUTPUT FILE-1
 6          MOVE ZERO TO REC-COUNTER
 7          PERFORM X-Ø1Ø-READ-FILE-1
 8          PERFORM X-Ø2Ø-READ-FILE-2
 9          PERFORM B-Ø1Ø-MATCH
10               UNTIL KEY-1 = KEY-2
11          PERFORM A-Ø3Ø-WRITE-RECORDS
12               UNTIL KEY-1 = HIGH-VALUES
13          DISPLAY 'TOTAL RECORDS WRITTEN IS' REC-COUNTER
14          CLOSE FILE-1 WITH LOCK
15                FILE-2 WITH LOCK
16                FILE-3 WITH LOCK
17          STOP RUN
18          .
19      A-Ø3Ø-WRITE-RECORDS.
20          MOVE FILE-1-REC TO FILE-3-REC
21          WRITE FILE-3-REC
22          MOVE FILE-2-REC TO FILE-3-REC
23          WRITE FILE-3-REC
24          ADD 2 TO REC-COUNTER
25          PERFORM X-Ø1Ø-READ-FILE-1
26          PERFORM B-Ø1Ø-MATCH
27               UNTIL KEY-1 = KEY-2
28          .
29    ***** LEVEL B *****
30      B-Ø1Ø-MATCH.
31          PERFORM X-Ø1Ø-READ-FILE-1
32               UNTIL KEY-1 NOT LESS THAN KEY-2
33          PERFORM X-Ø2Ø-READ-FILE-2
34               UNTIL KEY-2 NOT LESS THAN KEY-1
35          .
36    ***** LEVEL X *****
37      X-Ø1Ø-READ-FILE-1.
38          READ FILE-1
39               AT END MOVE HIGH-VALUES TO KEY-1
40          .
41      X-Ø2Ø-READ-FILE-2.
42          READ FILE-2
43               AT END MOVE HIGH-VALUES TO KEY-2
44          .
```

I have thrown in a few curves, so let us walk through it.

Lines 1, 29, and 36 are the level identifiers. New levels should
be started at the top of the source listing page by using EJECT (if your
compiler supports it).

Lines 2, 19, 30, 37, and 41 are the paragraph names. The first letter
indicates the level it is in; the three-digit number is the sequence number
of the paragraph within that level, and the balance of the paragraph name

would be off the VTOC if we had one. Since we do not, you make up the name.

Lines 1-10 is the beginning of job routine. Notice lines 9 and 10 force us to get a match before we hit the driver routine (lines 11 and 12).

Under our six rules for writing structured COBOL from scratch, rule three was initial reads. Maybe a more descriptive way of stating rule three is "before you hit the driver routine have the pump primed," or "the first thing accomplished in the driver routine should be the doing of it, not preparing to do" (where "it" is the purpose of the program).

The purpose (objective) of our program is to create an output file of matched records. Therefore, the first process in the driver module should be to create the file, not to prepare to create the file by reading and matching.

Lines 7 and 8 are performed routines because the reads of the input files are repetitive modules (executed from more than one place in the program).

Another good habit to get into is placing all your common I/O routines in the same level. It allows you to flip to one page and see them all. I made up a level "X" and placed them in it. Remember all other common modules are placed one level lower than the last level that performs them.

Notice I initialized the REC-COUNTER in the procedure division. Data that are variable should be initialized in the procedure division. Data that are constants (remain unchanged throughout the execution of the program) should be initialized in the working storage section. This helps in standardizing your programs. The match (B-Ø1Ø-MATCH) routine was placed in the B level since it is a repetitive module. (It's also executed in the A-Ø3Ø-WRITE-RECORDS paragraph.) If it had not been a repetitive module, we could have kept it in the A level since it is a PERFORM UNTIL (do until logic structure).

The driver routine (A-Ø3Ø-WRITE-RECORDS) is also a do until logic structure and since it is <u>not</u> large, complex, or repetitive, it can be left in the A level.

Notice the entire program is visible in the A level, and one struc- tured period terminates the top module.

Also observe that in A-Ø3Ø-WRITE-RECORDS (lines 25-27) the same "pump priming" functions are used that appeared in the beginning of the job. Again those are placed at the end of the paragraph.

Remember that COBOL's implementation of the iterative logic structure, the PERFORM UNTIL, <u>always checks the condition first</u>. Therefore, if the condition is already met before the PERFORM UNTIL is executed, the per- formed paragraph will not be executed even one time.

Notice, also, that only five structured periods are needed for the entire program and there is not an IF-ELSE in the program. This is due, in part, to the "power" of the PERFORM UNTIL COBOL verb.

Let's illustrate this by rewriting the program.

```
PROC DIV.
     OPEN INPUT YEC WHO OUTPUT BURP MOVE
     Ø TO C-1.
P-1. READ YEC END GO P-1Ø. READ WHO END
     GO P-1Ø.
P-2. IF X NOT = Y GO TO P-3 ELSE GO
     TO P-4.
P-3. IF X<Y GO P-6. IF Y<X GO TO
     P-7.
P-4. MOVE A TO B WRITE CX1 MOVE C
     TO B WRITE DX4 ADD 2 C-1 GO
     TO P-1
P-6. READ YEC END GO TO P-1Ø. IF
     X<Y GO TO P-6 ELSE IF X=Y
     GO TO P-4 ELSE IF X>Y GO TO
     P-7.
P-7. READ WHO AT END GO TO P-1Ø.IF
     Y<X GO TO P-7 ELSE IF X=Y
     GO TO P-4 ELSE IF Y>X GO TO
     P-6.
P-10. DISPLAY 'T.R.W.' C-1
      CLOSE YEC WHO BURP
      STOP RUN.
```

This example represents logic that does exactly the same thing the previous program does. That's where the similarity ends.

Advantage of Second Example

1) Uses less coding sheets or source statement library space.

Advantage of First Example

2) Uses descriptive data element names.
3) Uses descriptive paragraph names.
4) Adheres to indentation rules.
5) Does not abbreviate and take shortcuts.
6) Starts new lines with a verb.
7) Easy to understand.
8) Easy to maintain.
9) Longevity. (The next programmer who modifies your program will not come looking for you!)

We have now developed two methods of writing structured COBOL.

1) VTOC and/or HIPO ——▶ CODE

2) 6 RULES ——▶ CODE

We have further pointed out that writing the VTOC and/or HIPO first is probably the best method because of the usability of VTOCs and HIPOs as documentation and the value of VTOCs as a debugging tool.

One of the hardest things to get an understanding of in structured COBOL is having to "think" differently when designing programs.

- Top-down versus low-down
- Modularity versus blobularity
- Logic structures versus COBOLese
- Functional decomposition versus fermentation
- User involvement versus user harassment.

Old time COBOL programmers (10 plus years) adapting to structured techniques have it easy and hard at the same time. Old-timers tend to write structured code even though they do not call it that (they call it learning to write good code through experience). On the other hand, it is hard to develop new habits while breaking old ones if an "old-timer" has been writing unstructured code.

Structured COBOL will probably rule the world of coding when:

1) all of us old-timers die off
2) the universities teach structured methods, and
3) the languages are made more compatible with the structured methods.

If you are an old-timer and do not care to have to die off for the sake of the success of the structured revolution, this next section is for you.

Bridging the Generation Gap between Unstructured and Structured Code

or

How to Write Structured Code from Unstructured Code

or

How to Survive the Next War between the Go-Toers (pronounced 2ers, not toe-ers) and the Non Go-Toers

Consider this unstructured module.

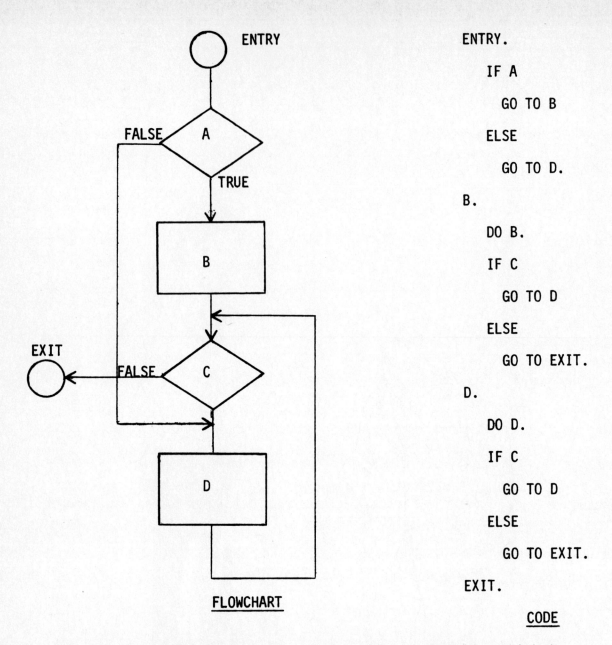

FLOWCHART

```
ENTRY.
   IF A
      GO TO B
   ELSE
      GO TO D.
B.
   DO B.
   IF C
      GO TO D
   ELSE
      GO TO EXIT.
D.
   DO D.
   IF C
      GO TO D
   ELSE
      GO TO EXIT.
EXIT.
```

CODE

The secret of structuring unstructured code is twofold: think in terms of logic structures, not COBOLese, and get to the exit as soon as possible. (Throughout this section, the verb DO can be replaced by the Cobol PERFORM.)

82

STRUCTURED

```
            ┌─────────────┐
            │             │
            │    ENTRY    │
            │             │
            └──────┬──────┘
                   │
   ┌───────┬───────┼───────┬───────────┐
 IF A   IF NOT A  UNTIL NOT C
┌────────┐┌────────┐┌────────┐┌────────┐
│        ││        ││        ││        │
│   B    ││   D    ││   D    ││  EXIT  │
│        ││        ││        ││        │
└────────┘└────────┘└────────┘└────────┘
```

IF A
    DO B
ELSE
    DO D
    .
DO D UNTIL NOT C
    .

VTOC   CODE

Being new at structuring unstructured code, your first effort
might proceed like this (coding from the flowchart).

You head for the EXIT as fast as you can get there (two-fold secret).

```
IF A
   DO B
   IF NOT C
      NEXT SENTENCE
      (You are out of the exit; next, match up the last unmatched IF
      and head for the exit again.)
   ELSE
      DO D UNTIL NOT C
      (You are out of the exit again.)
ELSE
   DO D
   IF NOT C
      NEXT SENTENCE
      (Out of the exit again)
   ELSE
      DO D UNTIL NOT C
```

Starting at the top again, think in terms of logic structures (one-
fold secret).

```
IF A
  DO B
```

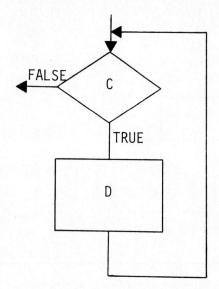

Notice that the above flowchart is a DO WHILE logic structure which is implemented in COBOL by the PERFORM UNTIL NOT verb.

Therefore, we can replace the:

```
IF NOT C
     NEXT SENTENCE
ELSE
     DO D UNTIL NOT C
by
     DO D UNTIL NOT C,
```

because the DO WHILE AND DO UNTIL logic structures <u>always</u> check the condition first. We now have:

```
IF A
  DO B
  DO D UNTIL NOT C
ELSE
  DO D
  DO D UNTIL NOT C
.
```

```
Or:   IF A
        DO B
      ELSE
        DO D
      .
      DO D UNTIL NOT C
      .
```

Here is another unstructured example to illustrate how we can get the final solution by just glancing at the unstructured module.

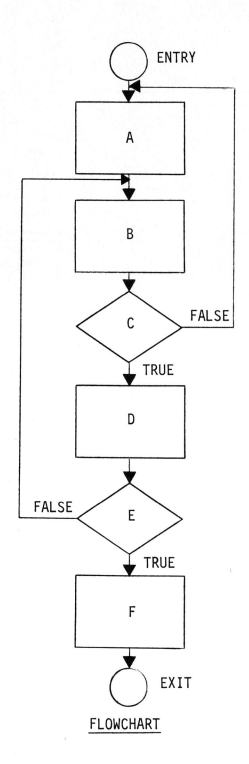

ENTRY

A

B

C   FALSE

TRUE

D

FALSE   E

TRUE

F

EXIT

FLOWCHART

```
ENTRY.
    DO A.
ENTRY-1
    DO B.
    IF C
        DO D
    ELSE
        GO TO ENTRY.
    IF E
        DO F
    ELSE
        GO TO ENTRY-1.
EXIT.
```

CODE

STRUCTURED

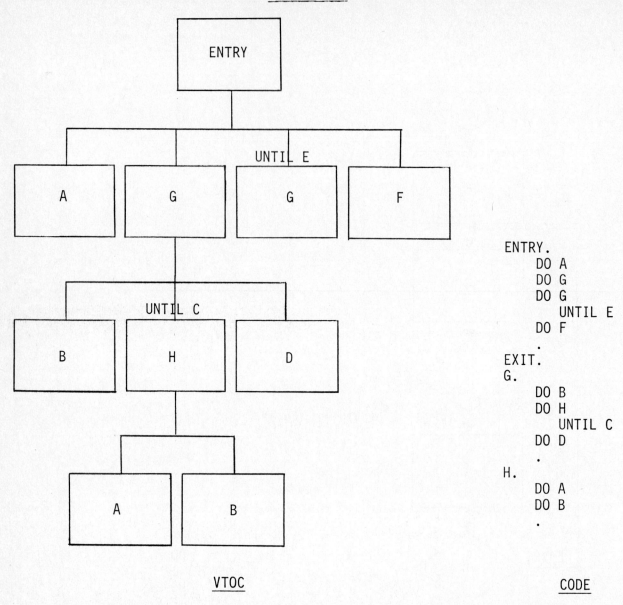

ENTRY.
 DO A
 DO G
 DO G
   UNTIL E
 DO F
 .
EXIT.
G.
 DO B
 DO H
   UNTIL C
 DO D
 .
H.
 DO A
 DO B
 .

VTOC   CODE

Here is how to combine one-fold and two-fold secrets at a glance.

Working from the flowchart again, what is the largest logic structure in it?

  - The largest one is a DO WHILE from condition E up to Process B.

Give it a name.

  - G.

How do you get down to it?

  - DO A
    DO G

How long do you want to do it?

- UNTIL E

What do you do after it's done?

- DO F

Put it all together.

- DO A
  DO G
  DO G UNTIL E
  DO F
  .

Now look at G.

What's the largest logic structure in it?

- From condition C up to process A.

Give it a name.

- H.

How do you get down to it?

- DO B

How long do you want to do it?

- UNTIL C.

What do you do after it's done?

- DO D.

Put it all together.

- G. DO B
      DO H UNTIL C
      DO D

Now look at H. What is the largest logic structure in it?

- DO A
  DO B

It is also the only logic structure in it, therefore:

- H. DO A
      DO B

Putting the three modules together, you have our solution.

One more example to illustrate how to go from unstructured to structured code is on the following page.

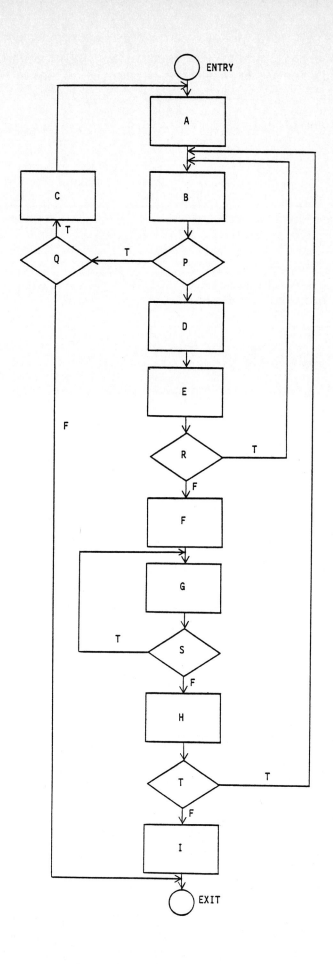

What is the largest logic structure in our ENTRY module? (Ignore the false side of condition Q for the time being; it is not a <u>legal</u> logic structure.)

- From condition T up to process B.

What do you want to call it?

- J

How do you get down to it?

```
- DO A
  DO J
```

How long do you want to do it?

- UNTIL NOT T

What do you do after it is done?

- DO I

Put it all together and you have the module ENTRY.

```
- ENTRY.
        DO A
        DO J
        DO J UNTIL NOT T
        DO I
          .
```

What is the largest logic structure within our J module?

- From condition R to process B

What do you want to call it?

- K

How do you get down to it?

- DO K

How long do you want to do it?

- UNTIL R

What do you do after it is done?

```
- DO F
  DO G
  DO G UNTIL NOT S
  DO H
```

Put it all together and you have J.

    - J.

            DO K
            DO K UNTIL R
            DO F
            DO G
            DO G UNTIL NOT S
            DO H
              .

What is the largest logic structure within K?

    - From condition P up to process A

What do you want to call it?

    - L

How do you get down to it?

    - DO B

How long do you want to do it?

    - UNTIL NOT P

What do you do after it is done?

    - DO D
    - DO E

Put it all together and you have K.

    - K.

            DO B
            DO L UNTIL NOT P
            DO D
            DO E
              .

What is the largest logic structure within L?

    - IF Q

            DO C
            DO A
            DO B
        ELSE
            GO TO EXIT

              .

What do you want to call it?

- It is all in-line expanded.

How do you get down to it?

- You start at the logic structure.

How long do you want to do it?

- It is not a loop.

What do you do after it is done?

- Go home.

Put it all together and you have L.

```
- L.  IF Q
          DO C
          DO A
          DO B
       ELSE
          GO TO EXIT
          .
```

This example illustrates that you can write such poor unstructured code (due to poor design), that you cannot structure it without completely redesigning and rewriting it.

G-15. Unstructured code that has more than one exit out of a logic structure cannot be structured. The module has to be redesigned.

In our example, our L module, which is within a DO WHILE logic structure, is an IF ELSE logic structure with a GO TO, which makes two exits: the false side of P and the false side of Q. Therefore, you have to use a GO TO to implement the module unless you redesign it.

Our complete program then looks like:

```
***** LEVEL A *****

    ENTRY.
        DO A                    (performed)
        DO J                    (performed)
        DO J UNTIL NOT T        (performed)
        DO I                    (in-line expanded)
              .
    EXIT.

***** LEVEL B *****

    J.
        DO K                    (performed)
        DO K UNTIL R            (performed)
        DO F                    (in-line expanded
        DO G                    (performed)
        DO G UNTIL NOT S        (performed)
        DO H                    (in-line expanded)

***** LEVEL C *****

    K.
        DO B                    (performed)
        DO L UNTIL NOT P        (performed on same level)
        DO D                    (in-line expanded)
        DO E                    (in-line expanded)
              .
    G.
    L.  IF Q                    (in-line expanded)
          DO C                  (in-line expanded)
          DO A                  (performed)
          DO B                  (performed)
        ELSE
          GO TO EXIT
              .

***** LEVEL D *****

    A.
    B.
```

In all our examples, we have simply applied our six rules to come up with our structured code (with the exception of our last example, which we cannot structure without redesigning).

To show once again that our six rules ≡ VTOC, as far as programming is concerned, the following VTOC represents our last example.

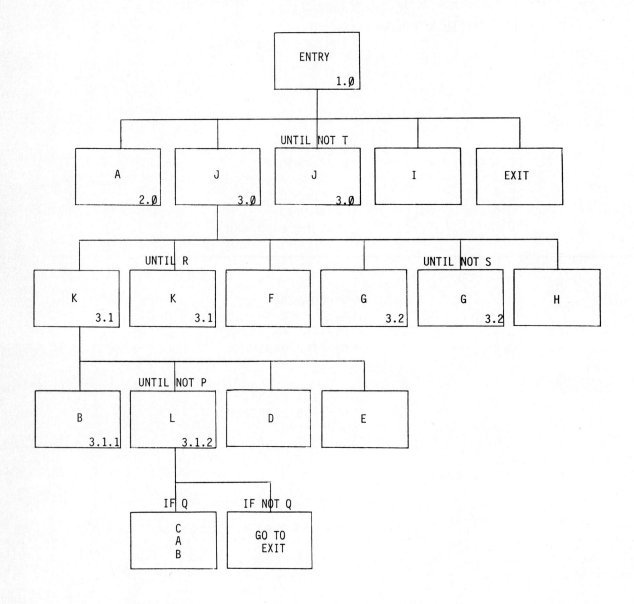

With the current design, the only way to avoid the GO TO is to set another switch when condition Q turns false, and then check it before executing the remaining modules. In other words, with this design, the cure is probably worse than the disease.

G-16. If a branch is absolutely necessary for clarity and understandability, for goodness' sake, use it.

In order to illustrate VTOCs, HIPOs,and programming with an example not as trivial as some of our first attempts, consider the following specifications. We will use sequential files again since multiple sequential files cause more problems in design than random access files.

Create a sequential tape file using 3 input files and an internal table.

1) INPUT FILE - 'FILE-1' - UNSORTED
    - SEQUENTIAL TAPE
    - FORMAT |ID-F1 | FIELD-A|

2) INPUT FILE - 'FILE-2' - SORTED
    - SEQUENTIAL TAPE
    - FORMAT |ID-F2 | FIELD-B OCCURS 10 TIMES|

3) INPUT-FILE - 'FILE-3' - ISAM
    - FORMAT |ID-F3 | FIELD-C|

4) INTERNAL TABLE - 'TABLE-4' - SORTED
    - 1000 OCCURENCES
    - FORMAT |ID-F4 | FIELD-D|

5) OUTPUT FILE - 'FILE-5'
    - SEQUENTIAL TAPE
    - FORMAT |ID-F5 | FIELD-AO | FIELD-BO occurs 10 times | FIELD-CO
               | FIELD-DO |

6) All files and table are keyed on ID-F(N)

7) Output record is created if ID-F1 = ID-F2

8) Omit all FILE-1 records with FIELD-A = '999'

9) FILE-3 RECORD MAY NOT EXIST, IF IT DOESN'T, USE SPACES FOR FIELD-CO.

10) 'TABLE-4' RECORD MAY NOT EXIST, IF IT DOESN'T, USE SPACES FOR FIELD-DO.

11) Use ID-F(N), FIELD-A, FIELD-B, FIELD-C's, and FIELD-D to create FILE-5.
    (KEY-F(N), FIELD-A, FIELD-B are mandatory; FIELD-C, FIELD-D are optional.)

12) FIELD-B in FILE-2 occurs 10 times and you only use B FIELDS that are numeric;
    else update 'FIELD-BO' with zeroes.

13) NO EDITING OR PRINTED REPORTS

14) SORT FILE-1 internally.

15) Use SEARCH-ALL for TABLE lookup.

16) Use subscripts for FILE-2.

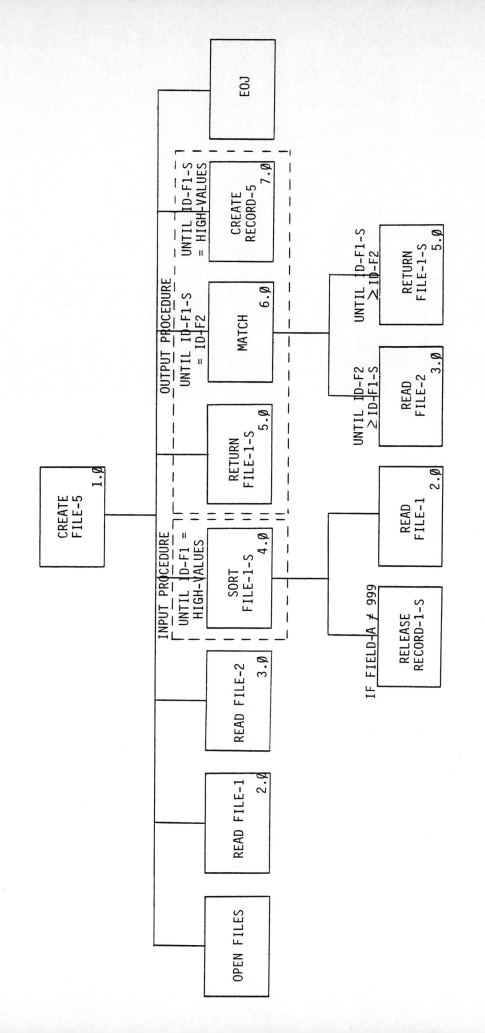

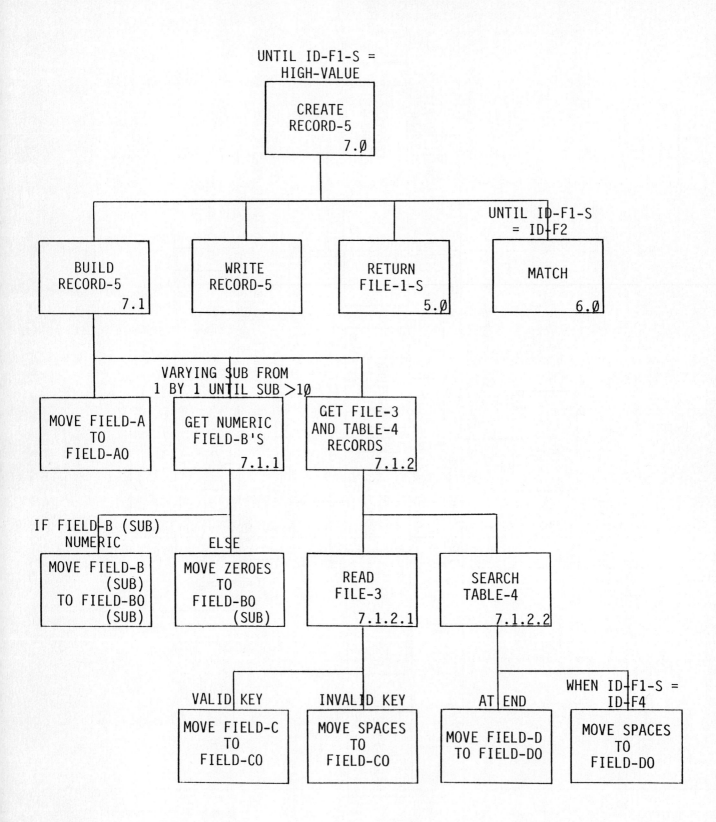

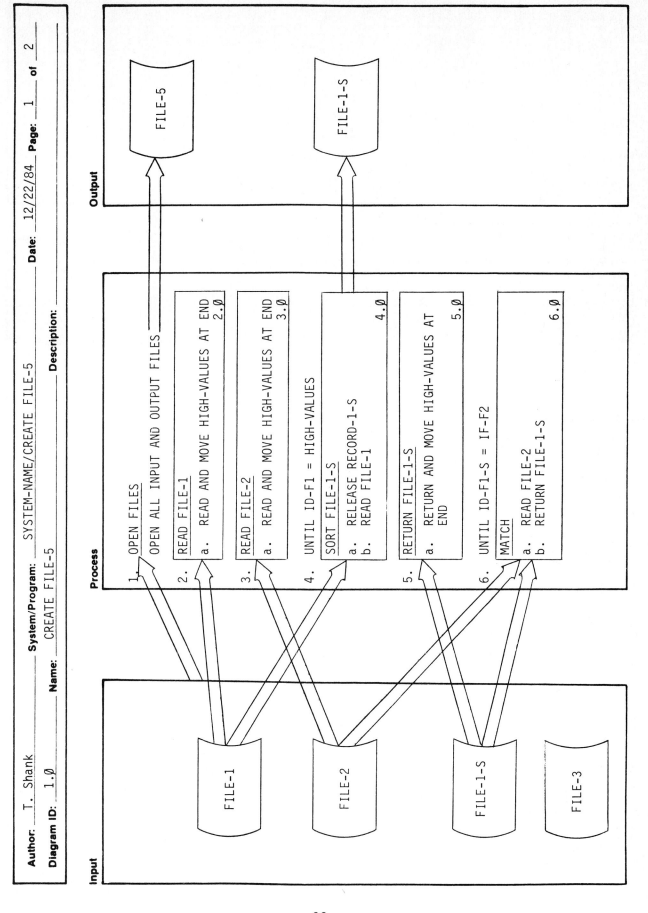

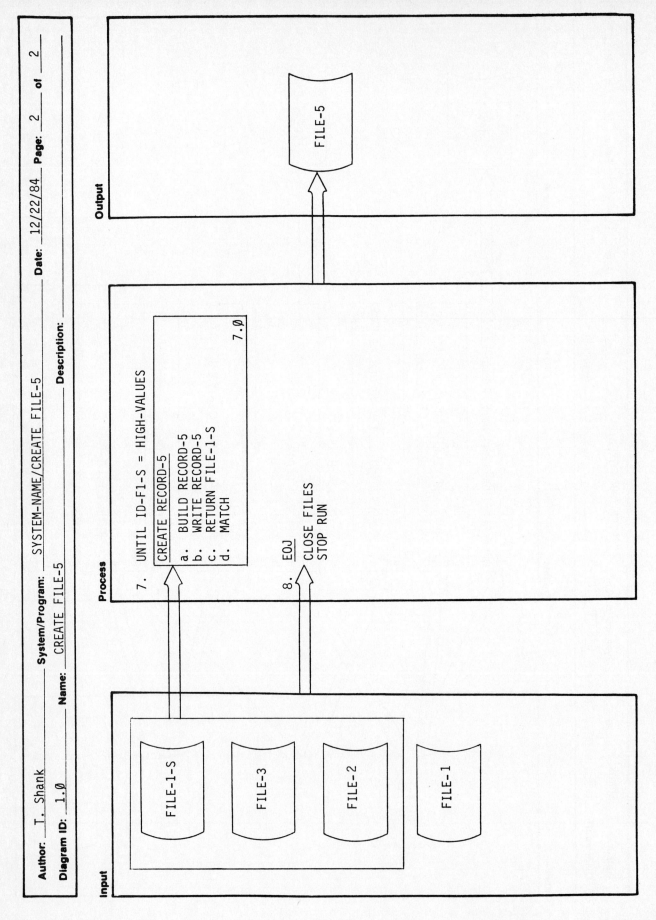

Input

FILE-1-S

FILE-3

FILE-2

FILE-1

Process

7. UNTIL ID-F1-S = HIGH-VALUES

CREATE RECORD-5

a. BUILD RECORD-5
b. WRITE RECORD-5
c. RETURN FILE-1-S
d. MATCH

7.0

8. EOJ

CLOSE FILES
STOP RUN

Output

FILE-5

100

FILE-1 FILE DESCRIPTION

VOLUME LABEL IS CØ1.
HEADER LABEL IS 'FILE-1,' 99/999.
BLOCKING FACTOR IS 1ØØØ.
RECORD LENGTH IS 7.
MEDIA IS DATA CELL.
FILE IS SEQUENTIALLY ORGANIZED ON 4-DIGIT KEY.
FILE IS UPDATED BY SYS-NAM Ø6, SYS-NAM 1Ø.

FILE-2 FILE DESCRIPTION

VOLUME LABEL IS F12.
HEADER LABEL IS 'FILE-2.'
BLOCKING FACTOR IS 1ØØ.
RECORD LENGTH IS 34.
MEDIA IS DRUM.
FILE IS SEQUENTIALLY ORGANIZED ON 4-DIGIT KEY.
FILE IS UPDATED BY SYS-NAME 15, SYS-NAME 2Ø.

FILE-3 FILE DESCRIPTION

VOLUME LABEL IS A11.
HEADER LABEL IS 'FILE-3.'
BLOCKING FACTOR IS 1.
RECORD LENGTH IS 7.
MEDIA IS DISK.
FILE IS INDEXED AND SEQUENTIALLY ORGANIZED ON 4-DIGIT KEY.
FILE IS NEVER UPDATED.

FILE-5 FILE DESCRIPTION

VOLUME LABEL IS A22.
HEADER LABEL IS 'FILE-5.'
BLOCKING FACTOR IS 1ØØ.
RECORD LENGTH IS 43.
MEDIA IS TAPE.
FILE IS SEQUENTIALLY ORGANIZED ON 4-DIGIT KEY.
FILE IS CREATED BY CREATE FILE-5 AND IS NEVER UPDATED.

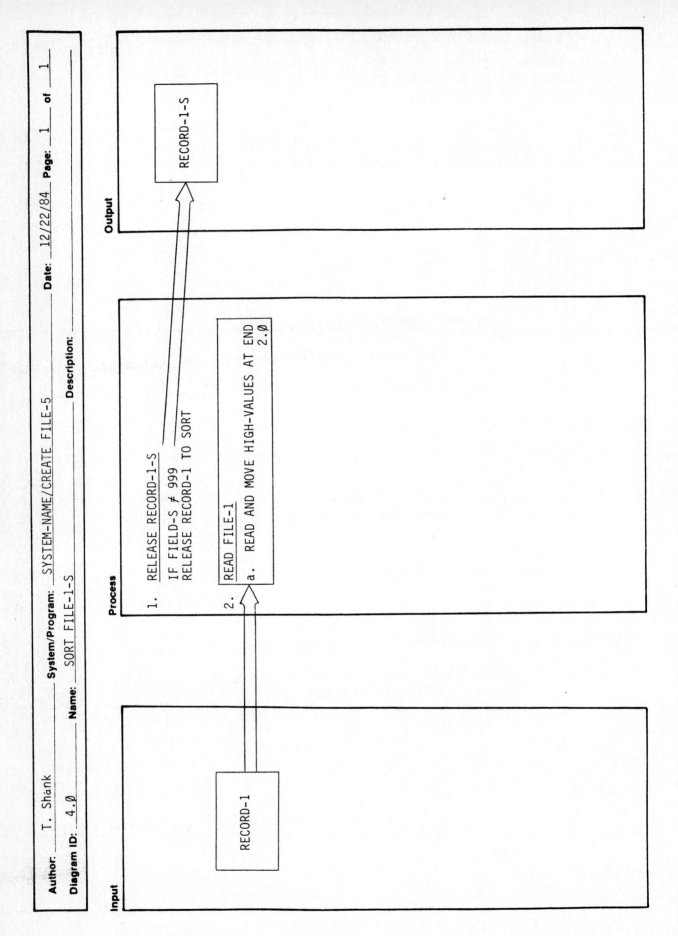

Output

RECORD-1-S

Process

1. RELEASE RECORD-1-S

    IF FIELD-S ≠ 999
    RELEASE RECORD-1 TO SORT

2. READ FILE-1
   a. READ AND MOVE HIGH-VALUES AT END   2.0

Input

RECORD-1

FILE-1-S FILE DESCRIPTION

VOLUME LABEL IS A15.
HEADER LABEL IS 'SORT WK 1' THROUGH 'SORT WK 3'.
BLOCKING FACTOR IS 1.
RECORD LENGTH IS 7.
MEDIA IS DISK.
FILE IS AN SD USED ONLY BY CREATE FILE-5.
SELECT CLAUSE MUST USE SYS NUMBERS ØØ1 THROUGH ØØ3 (E.G., SYSØØ1, SYSØØ2, SYSØØ3).

FILE-1-S RECORD DESCRIPTION

| ID-F1-S | FIELD-A-S |

ID-F1-S IS A 4 CHARACTER ALPHA-NUMERIC FIELD. USAGE IS DISPLAY. THIS IS THE
SORT KEY.
FIELD-A-S IS A 3 CHARACTER ALPHA-NUMERIC FIELD. USAGE IS DISPLAY.
RECORD LENGTH IS 7.

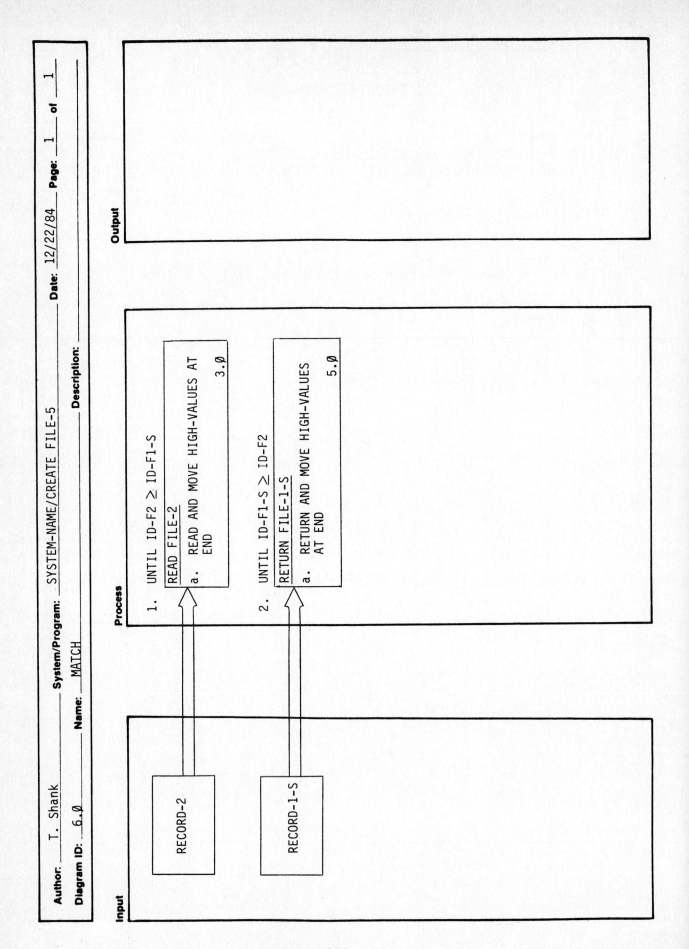

Input   **Process**   **Output**

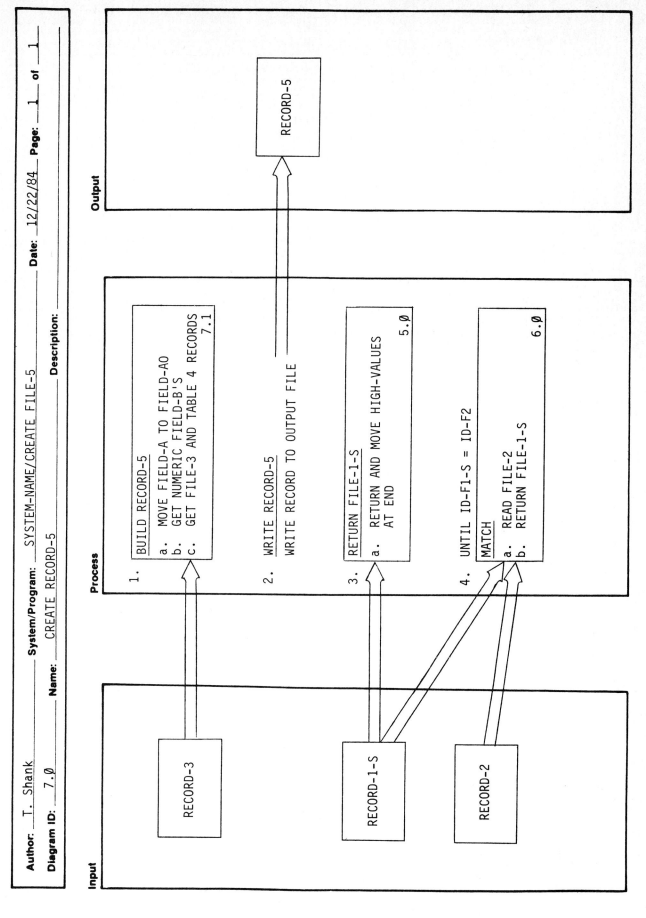

1. BUILD RECORD-5   7.1
   a. MOVE FIELD-A TO FIELD-AO
   b. GET NUMERIC FIELD-B'S
   c. GET FILE-3 AND TABLE 4 RECORDS

2. WRITE RECORD-5
   WRITE RECORD TO OUTPUT FILE

3. RETURN FILE-1-S   5.0
   a. RETURN AND MOVE HIGH-VALUES
       AT END

4. UNTIL ID-F1-S = ID-F2   6.0
   MATCH
   a. READ FILE-2
   b. RETURN FILE-1-S

RECORD-5

RECORD-3

RECORD-1-S

RECORD-2

RECORD-5 RECORD DESCRIPTION

| IF-F5 | FIELD-AO | FIELD-BO OCCURS 10 TIMES | FIELD-CO | FIELD-DO |

ID-F4 is a four-character, alphanumeric key field.

FIELD-AO, FIELD-BO, FIELD-CO, FIELD-DO are all three-character alphanumeric fields. FIELD-BO occurs ten times.

Record length is 43.

Author: T. Shank **System/Program:** SYSTEM-NAME/CREATE-FILE-5 **Date:** 12/22/84 **Page:** 1 **of** 1

Diagram ID: 7.1.1. **Name:** GET NUMERIC FIELD-B'S **Description:**

Input

Process

1. <u>MOVE FIELD-B TO FIELD-BO</u>

   IF FIELD-B (SUB) IS NUMERIC
   MOVE FIELD-B (SUB) TO
   FIELD-BO (SUB)

2. <u>MOVE ZEROES TO FIELD-BO</u>

   IF FIELD-B (SUB) IS NOT
   NUMERIC MOVE ZEROES
   TO FIELD-BO

Output

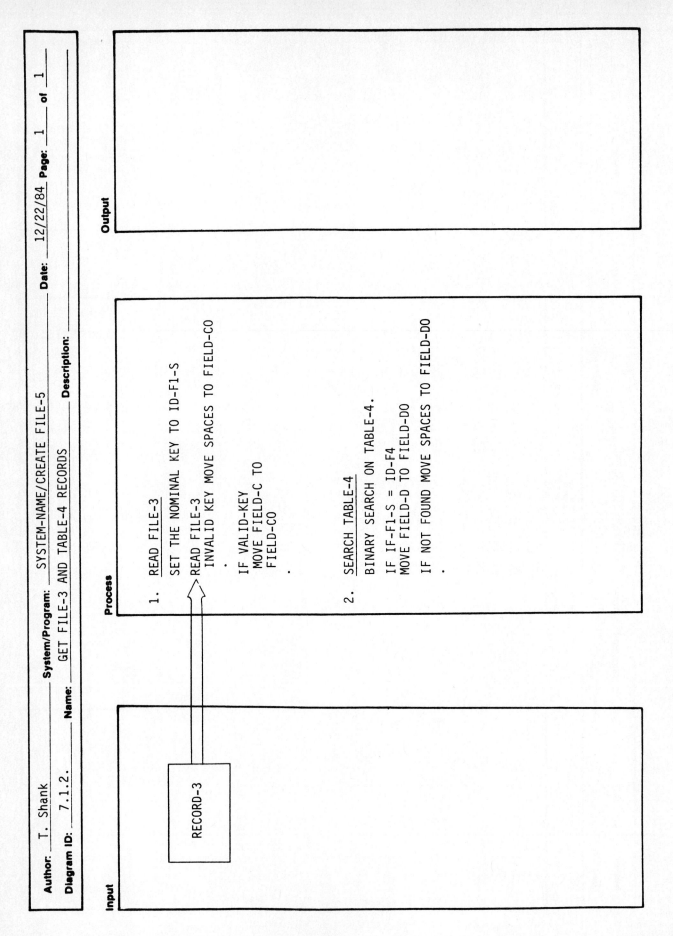

Output

Process

1. READ FILE-3
   SET THE NOMINAL KEY TO ID-F1-S

   READ FILE-3
   INVALID KEY MOVE SPACES TO FIELD-CO
   .

   IF VALID-KEY
   MOVE FIELD-C TO
   FIELD-CO
   .

2. SEARCH TABLE-4
   BINARY SEARCH ON TABLE-4.

   IF IF-F1-S = ID-F4
   MOVE FIELD-D TO FIELD-DO

   IF NOT FOUND MOVE SPACES TO FIELD-DO
   .

RECORD-3

Input

RECORD-3 RECORD DESCRIPTION

|ID-F3 | FIELD-C|

ID-F3 is a four-character alphanumeric key field.

FIELD-C is a three-character alphanumeric field.

Record length is 7.

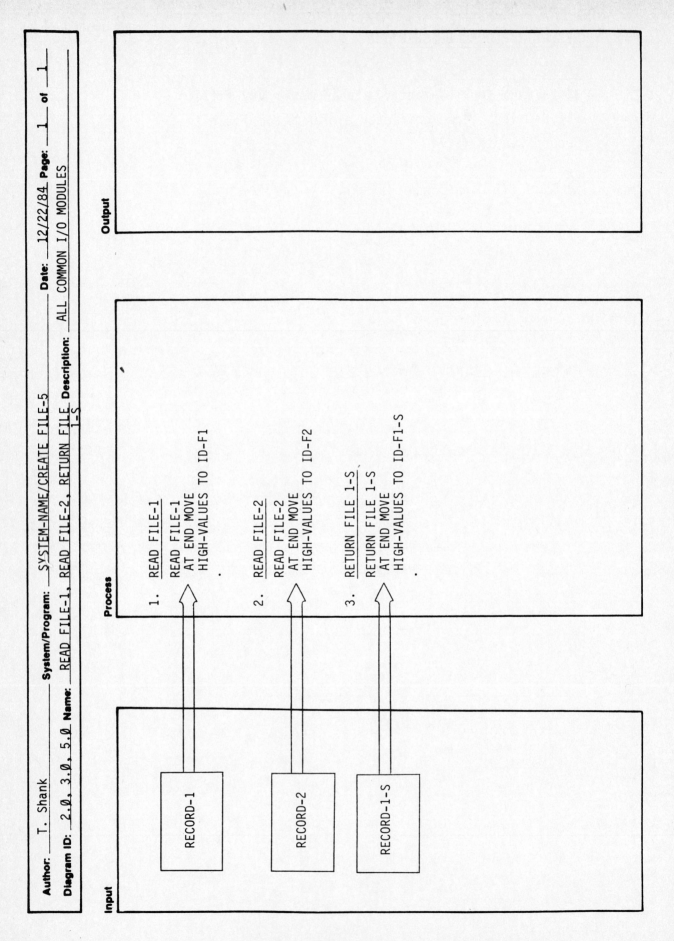

Output

Process

1. READ FILE-1

   READ FILE-1
   AT END MOVE
   HIGH-VALUES TO ID-F1
   .

2. READ FILE-2

   READ FILE-2
   AT END MOVE
   HIGH-VALUES TO ID-F2
   .

3. RETURN FILE 1-S

   RETURN FILE 1-S
   AT END MOVE
   HIGH-VALUES TO ID-F1-S
   .

Input

RECORD-1

RECORD-2

RECORD-1-S

110

RECORD-1 RECORD DESCRIPTION

|ID-F1 | FIELD-A|

ID-F1 is a four-character alphanumeric key field.

FIELD-A is a three-character alphanumeric field.

Record length is 7.

RECORD-2 RECORD DESCRIPTION

|ID-F2 | FIELD-B | OCCURS 10 TIMES|

ID-F2 is a four-character alphanumeric key field.

FIELD-BO is a three-character alphanumeric field which occurs ten times.

Record length is 34.

RECORD-1-S RECORD DESCRIPTION

See record description under 4.0.

```
***** LEVEL A *****

A-Ø1Ø-CREATE- FILE-5-1Ø
    OPEN INPUT FILE-1
                FILE-2
                FILE-3
         OUTPUT FILE-5
    PERFORM X-Ø1Ø-READ-FILE-1-2Ø
    PERFORM X-Ø2Ø-READ-FILE-2-3Ø
    SORT FILE-1-S ON ASCENDING KEY ID-F1-S
         INPUT PROCEDURE IS B-Ø1Ø-SORT-FILE-4Ø
         OUTPUT PROCEDURE IS B-Ø2Ø-RET-MATCH-CREATE-50-60-70
    CLOSE FILE-1
          FILE-2
          FILE-3
          FILE-5
    STOP RUN
    .




***** LEVEL B *****

B-Ø1Ø-SORT-FILE-4Ø SECTION.
    PERFORM B-Ø3Ø-RELEASE-READ-2Ø
        UNTIL ID-F1 = HIGH-VALUES
    .
B-Ø2Ø-RET-MATCH-CREATE-5Ø-6Ø-7Ø SECTION.
    PERFORM X-Ø3Ø-RETURN-1-5Ø
    PERFORM C-Ø1Ø-READ-2-RETURN-1-3Ø-5Ø
        UNTIL ID-F1-S = ID-F2
    PERFORM B-Ø4Ø-CREATE-REC-5-7Ø
        UNTIL ID-F1-S = HIGH-VALUES
    .
B-Ø2Ø-EXIT SECTION.

B-Ø3Ø-RELEASE-READ-2Ø.
    IF FIELD-A NOT = 999
        RELEASE RECORD-1-S
    .
    PERFORM X-Ø1Ø-READ-FILE-1-2Ø
    .
B-Ø4Ø-CREATE-REC-5-7Ø
    PERFORM C-Ø2Ø-BUILD-RECORD-71
    WRITE FILE-5
    PERFORM X-Ø3Ø-RETURN-1-5Ø
    PERFORM C-Ø1Ø-READ-2-RETURN-1-3Ø-5Ø
        UNTIL ID-F1-S = ID-F2
    .
```

```
***** LEVEL C *****

C-Ø1Ø-READ-2-RETURN-1-3Ø-5Ø.
     PERFORM X-Ø2Ø-READ-FILE-2-3Ø
          UNTIL ID-F2 NOT LESS THAN ID-F1-S
     PERFORM X-Ø3Ø-RETURN-1-5Ø
          UNTIL ID-F1-S NOT LESS THAN ID-F2
       .

C-Ø1Ø-BUILD-RECORD-71.
     MOVE FIELD-A TO FIELD-AO
     MOVE ID-F1-S TO ID-F5
     PERFORM D-Ø1Ø-GET-NUM-FIELDS-711
          VARYING SUB FROM 1 BY 1
               UNTIL SUB71Ø
     PERFORM D-Ø2Ø-GET-3-4-RECORDS-712
       .




***** LEVEL D *****

D-Ø1Ø-GET-NUM-FIELDS-711.
    IF FIELD-B (SUB) NUMERIC
        MOVE FIELD-B (SUB) TO
             FIELD-BO (SUB)
    ELSE
        MOVE ZEROES TO FIELD-BO (SUB)
      .

D-Ø2Ø-GET-3-4-RECORDS-712.
    READ FILE-3
        INVALID KEY
            MOVE SPACES TO FIELD-CO
      .
    IF ID-F1-S = ID-F3
        MOVE FIELD-C TO FIELD-CO
      .
    SEARCH ALL TABLE-4
        AT END
            MOVE SPACES TO FIELD-DO
        WHEN ID-F1-S = ID-F4
            MOVE FIELD-D TO FIELD-DO
      .
```

```
***** LEVEL X *****

X-Ø1Ø-READ-FILE-1-2Ø.
     READ FILE-1
          AT END MOVE HIGH-VALUES TO ID-F1
     .

X-Ø2Ø-READ-FILE-2-3Ø.
     READ FILE-2
          AT END MOVE HIGH-VALUES TO ID-F2
     .

X-Ø3Ø-RETURN-1-5Ø.
     RETURN FILE-1-S
          AT END MOVE HIGH-VALUES TO ID-F1-S
     .
```

I have purposely used excessively detailed paragraph names and HIPOs to illustrate all of the techniques we have discussed. You might want to HIPO only those COBOL paragraphs that need additional definition before coding.

This example can serve as a model when using subscripting, searches, sorts, or random file processing.

Notice that our "pump priming" included a match routine because we wanted to build and write the record first in our driver module. Remember to identify the purpose of the program (create a file), then have every-thing ready to accomplish this purpose (create first record) when you execute the driver (create record-5) for the first time.

Also notice that the files and records were described as they "fell out of the design." In other words, it was when the modules, using or creating them, were down to the pseudo-code.

An extremely important concept to get a grasp of is recognizing the difference between conditions and processes. Realizing, for instance, that the two processes in sort-f-1-s are release a record and read a record, it allows you to create the structure first and then place conditions where they belong.

Let us look at the four primary and four secondary principles of design we developed in the section on VTOCs to see if there is any applicability to this example. Admittedly, some of the design principles are difficult to apply at the program level due to the restraints of the program language, but the essence of the principle is retained.

Top-Down: obviously applicable.

Modular Design: It is definitely modular, but we do not know how good the modules are until we put the cohesion and coupling test on them.

Functional Decomposition: obviously applicable.

114

User Involvement: The system designer is probably the user; he should be involved in the program design.

Cohesion: If you recall, we had two definitions for high cohesion. A) Functional (high) cohesion is the absence of the first six cohesions. B) Functional (high) cohesion is the cohesion you get when the user designs his own system.

The obvious conclusion is to get users to design their own programs (love it!). If that fails, see if you can design program modules getting as close to functional cohesion as possible.

Picking a module out of our example, say 7.0 (<u>create record-5</u>), let's run thru (COBOL through) the seven cohesions to see which one fits the best.

Since there is an obvious reason for grouping the four functions together (build, write, return, and match) within <u>create record-5</u>, this module is not coincidentally cohesive.

It is definitely not logically cohesive. (That would mean grouping all of our I/O in one module, all of our editing in one module, etc.)

Even though the functions within <u>create record-5</u> happen within a few nanoseconds of each other (depending on your hardware configuration), it is not temporally cohesive because we did not design the module around any time considerations.

It certainly could be procedurally cohesive since the four functions accomplish a certain task: creating a record. This, however, does not mean it cannot be functionally cohesive also, since procedural cohesion can be a subset (including the whole set) of functional cohesion.

Since we are not doing <u>all</u> of the processing on each record in one place, and it was not even our intent to do so, we do not have communicational cohesion.

The output from the write function is not the input for the return module; therefore, it is not sequentially cohesive.

Unless this dude is procedurally cohesive, we <u>must</u> have functional cohesion.

I have noticed something in system/subsystem/program design using VTOCs that is worthy of another "G" number.

G-17. The top modules in your MIS design (if MIS is not a figment of our imagination) are easy to make functionally cohesive. The bottom modules in a program are easy to make functionally cohesive. The intermediate levels are the ones that are tough.

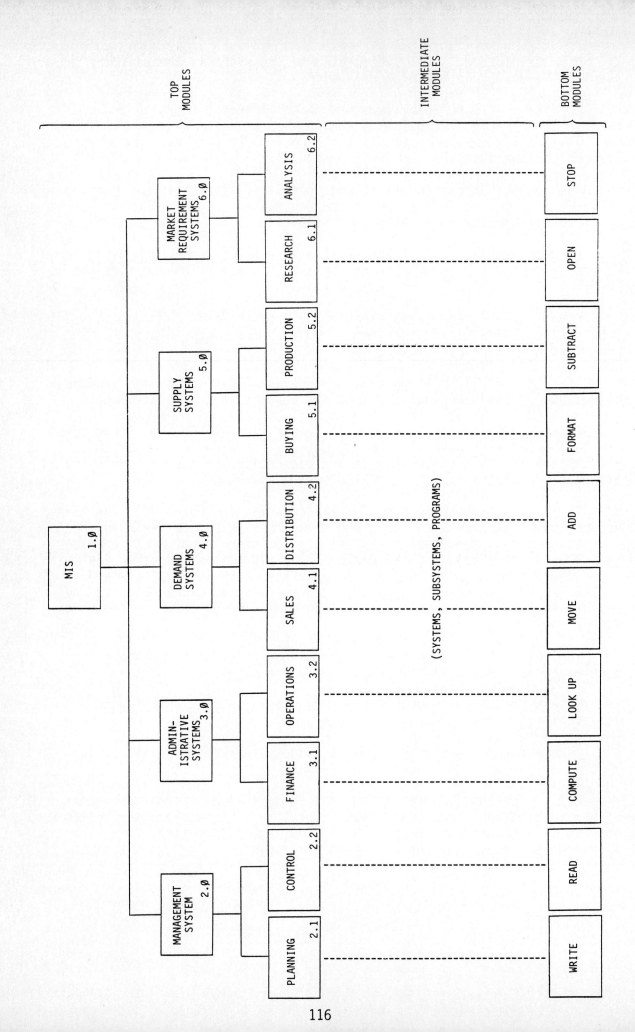

Since so many MIS's are built around the organizational structure, the top modules are functional by definition. COBOL instructions are also functional by definition (although compiler writers might beg to differ). Anyway, back to our example. I would rank each of our modules thusly.

ALL BOTTOM MODULES   - 7
SORT FILE-1-S   - 4 or 7
MATCH   - 4 or 7
CREATE RECORD-5   - 4 or 7
EOJ   - 3
BUILD RECORD-5   - 4 or 7
GET NUMERIC B-FIELDS   - 7
GET FILE-3 AND TABLE-4 RECORDS - 1, 2, or 3
READ FILE-3   - 7
SEARCH TABLE-4   - 7

Where 1 = coincidental cohesion
      2 = logical cohesion
      3 = temporal cohesion
      4 = procedural cohesion
      5 = communicational cohesion
      6 = sequential cohesion
      7 = functional cohesion

If cohesion was our only criterion for measuring design strength, probably our weakest module is GET FILE-3 AND TABLE-4 RECORDS (which does look a little weak; why group those functions together?).

Coupling: We have kept our conditions outside the process and have no duplicate modules other than the initial read tape modules (pump priming).

Span of Control: We have one function decomposed into more than six functions - the create file-5 module. We could cut this back to six if you introduced a BOJ module.

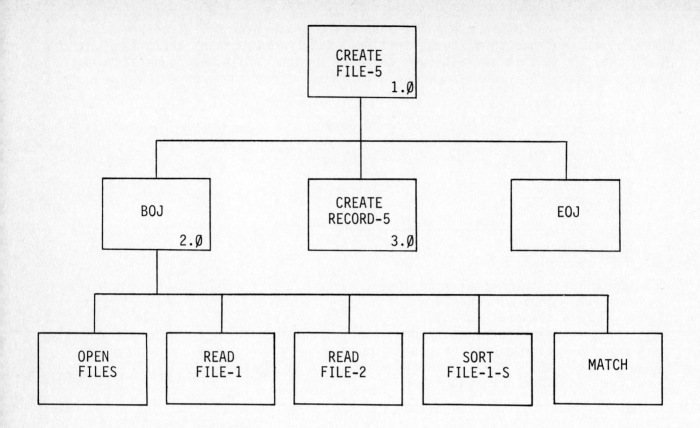

(I am not too crazy about that since I like to see all the BOJ code in level A.)

Amount of Detail: All of our bottom modules are to the point where we can envision how to implement them in COBOL. The only difficulty might be _too_ much detail.

The dotted lines on the VTOC indicate the paragraphs that must be logically within the input or output procedures due to the presence of RELEASE AND RETURN verbs.

We have now designed programs that use a wide variety of COBOL verbs. As a final illustration, let's consider a complex (not necessarily large) program.

If you can solve this problem with or without VTOCs, you are probably in the 30K plus salary range.

SPECS

- Make one sequential input master file.
- Make one sequential input transaction file.
- Update the master file with the transaction file, creating a sequential output master file.
- Have both files presorted on a key.
- A transaction record without a matching master record indicates an add.
- An equal key on both files indicates a change unless the transaction record has a delete code, in which case it is a delete.

- The master file has no duplicate records.
- The transaction file can have one or more records with the same key.
- Other than the key, the transaction file is not sorted on any other field.

The following test data will illustrate the specifications.

Master Records	Transaction Records
1	2
4	4
6	4-DEL
10	4
12	5
16	5
17	5-DEL
18	7
	11
	13
	16-DEL
	16
	17
	18
	18

In this example, for instance, the master 1 record is written out as is, the transaction 2 record is an add, the first transaction 4 record updates the master 4 record, the next transaction 4 record deletes it, the next transaction 4 record re-adds it, the first transaction 5 record is an add, the next one is a change, and the next a delete (therefore the output master file never ends up with a 5 record), and so on .... .

If you can VTOC this logic, you can VTOC any logic.

Give it a whirl before you look at my solution (there are, of course, many solutions).

If you can solve the algorithm in less than an hour, and you are looking for work, let me know.

To help you get started, I will solve the first level for you.

```
+-----------------+
|    UPDATE       |
|   PROGRAM       |
|                 |
|       1.0       |
+-----------------+
```

119

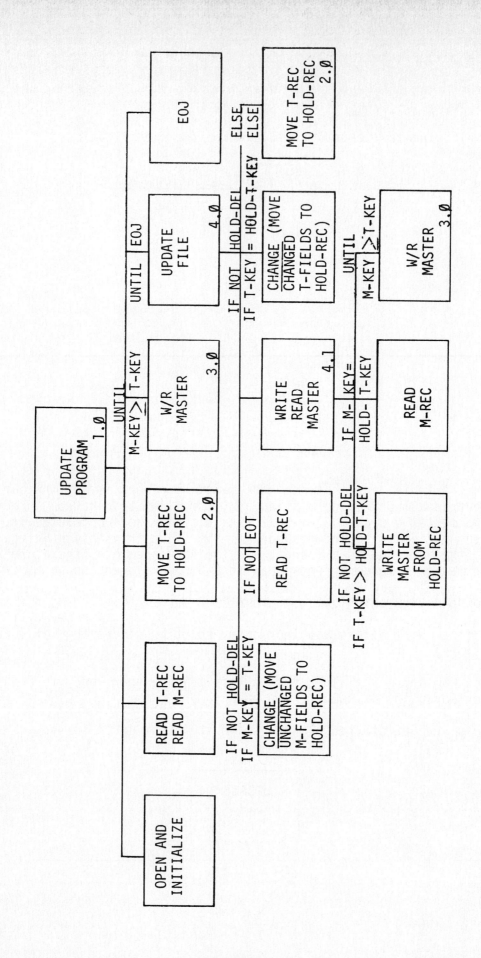

120

Hold-Rec, Hold-Del, and Hold-T-Key are working storage areas.

I also assumed the transaction and master records had identical formats which allowed me to move the unchanged master fields into the transaction record in working storage. Remember also to move HIGH-VALUES to your T-Key and M-Key when the files go to AT END.

G-17. The I/O in sequential file processing that has duplicate keys on the transaction file can be handled by placing the <u>read trans</u>, <u>write master from hold area</u>, <u>read master</u>, <u>write/read master from the FD</u>, and <u>move trans to hold area</u> at the end of the level in that order.

STRUCTURED TESTING

If the VTOC, HIPOs and structured programming tools we have discussed so far only whet your appetite for law and order in application
programming, I would highly recommend the following additional structured
tools that support structured programming.

Structured testing is a tool that allows you to test your program
the same way you designed it - - top-down by module.

Assume the following VTOC is our finished program.

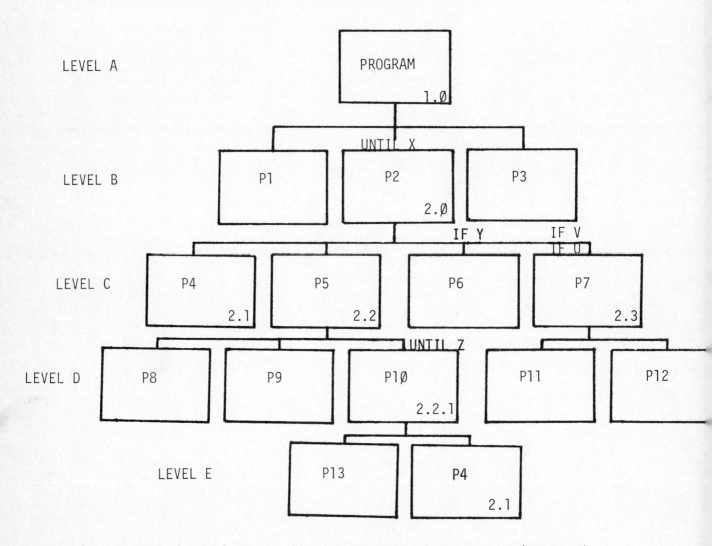

In structured testing, you test the top level by itself (level A).
When that code works, you add level B and test level A and B together.
If A and B work, add C; test all three, and continue this process until
you reach the bottom of the design.

In our example, the format of level A would be:

```
***** LEVEL A *****

A-Ø1Ø-PROGRAM-1Ø.
        ┌ CODE
     P1 ┤ CODE
        └ CODE

        PERFORM B-Ø1Ø-P2-2Ø
             UNTIL X

        ┌ CODE
     P3 ┤ CODE
        └ CODE


             .
```

Even though we don't code level B, it's immediately obvious that
if we don't include paragraph name B-Ø1Ø-P2-2Ø our program won't compile.
Coding in lower level paragraph names is called dummying (or stubbing) in
the lower modules.

This is not the end of it however. What would happen if I included
a B level paragraph (B-Ø1Ø-P2-2Ø) recompiled (got a clean compile) and ran
a test?

That's right - - - - nothing. You would get in an infinite loop unless condition X gets set in the B-Ø1Ø-P2-2Ø paragraph.

And finally, how do you know the bottom modules (stubs) are being
executed and in the proper order?

```
***** LEVEL A *****

A-Ø1Ø-PROGRAM-1Ø.
         ⎧ CODE
    P1   ⎨ CODE
         ⎩ CODE

         PERFORM B-Ø1Ø-P2-2Ø
            UNTIL X

         ⎧ CODE
    P3   ⎨ CODE
         ⎩ CODE

          .


***** LEVEL B *****

B-Ø1Ø-P2-2Ø.                     ──────────→ Stub
     DISPLAY 'B-Ø1Ø-P2-2Ø' ──────────→ I Made It
     SET    X    TRUE      ──────────→ Set Switch

      .
```

When the program is tested, the output for a successful run would be:

B-Ø1Ø-P2-2Ø.

Adding level B our program expands to:

```
***** LEVEL A *****

A-Ø1Ø-PROGRAM-1Ø.
         ⎧ CODE
    P1   ⎨ CODE
         ⎩ CODE

         PERFORM B-Ø1Ø-P2-2Ø
            UNTIL X

         ⎧ CODE
    P3   ⎨ CODE
         ⎩ CODE

          .
```

```
***** LEVEL B *****

B-Ø1Ø-P2-20.
      PERFORM X-Ø1Ø-P4-21
      PERFORM C-Ø1Ø-P5-22
      IF Y
      ⌈ CODE
P6    ⎨ CODE
      ⌊ CODE
          .

      IF V
      IF U
       PERFORM C-Ø2Ø-P7-23
          .

***** LEVEL C *****

C-Ø1Ø-P5-22.
      DISPLAY 'C-Ø1Ø-P5-22'
          .

C-Ø2Ø-P7-23.
      DISPLAY 'CØ2Ø-P7-23'
          .

***** LEVEL X *****

X-Ø1Ø-P4-21.
      DISPLAY 'X-Ø1Ø-P4-21'
          .
```

A test at this level should give you:

```
      X-Ø1Ø-P4-21
      C-Ø1Ø-P5-22
      C-Ø2Ø-P7-23.
```

Any printed output from the in-line expanded modules would also be interspersed with your displays.

Level C is the last level before the program is complete.

```
***** LEVEL C *****

C-Ø1Ø-P5-22.

          ⌠CODE
P8      ⎨CODE
          ⌡CODE

          ⌠CODE
P9      ⎨CODE
          ⌡CODE

       PERFORM D-Ø1Ø-P1Ø-221
            UNTIL Z

          ⌠CODE
P11     ⎨CODE
          ⌡CODE

          ⌠CODE
P12     ⎨CODE
          ⌡CODE
        .

***** LEVEL D *****

D-Ø1Ø-P1Ø-221.
     DISPLAY 'D-Ø1Ø-P1Ø-221'
     SET Z TO TRUE
        .

***** LEVEL X *****

X-Ø1Ø-P4-21.
     DISPLAY 'X-Ø1Ø-P4-21'
        .
```

One obvious advantage in testing a program by levels is the ability
to locate bugs more readily. When the first test of a program includes all of
the code, it is very difficult (especially in large programs) to isolate
the errors. If the program is tested top-down, the moment a bug is encountered you know what level it is on (the level you are testing) and the
logic error is found much more easily.

Another advantage of structured testing is the ability to spread out
your test time over the length of the project, thereby avoiding a big
computer time crunch when everyone wants to test at the same time.

How many times have you thought your program had a bug when all along
it was the software controlling your program that was in error (JCL, OCL,
or whatever you call it)? Notice that in order to test level A, the JCL
has to be correct. Since level A is generally a simple level to test,
this is an excellent time to find all of your JCL bugs.

The most frequently executed modules in a production program are the top level modules (lower level modules may never be executed if a condition keeps them from executing). In top-down testing, the most frequently tested modules (Test A, Test A & B, Test A & B & C, etc.) are the modules which will be executed most often in a production environment.

Another advantage I have observed in top-down testing is a result of encountering logic errors one at a time. Many times an error is the result of more than one bug. A systematic method of uncovering bugs allows you to fix them one at a time without becoming involved in unraveling a maze of interrelated problems.

Finally, if certain modules have not been defined yet, structured testing allows you to progress with your testing and the undefined modules can be coded as stubs.

Please notice that structured testing does not preclude writing the entire program at one setting. Your coding efforts can run ahead of your testing.

Like any other structured tool, structured testing can get in the way of production if abused (e.g., I wouldn't test a simple two-level program top-down). The way to find out where structured testing can enhance production is to try it out on several programs and learn by experience what type of projects top-down testing is best suited. No structured tool should be used as an end in itself but as an aid in increasing productivity.

A neat extension of structured program testing is to move the concept to the system level. Your stubs become programs and subsystems instead of paragraphs and you can dummy in program names in your program libraries. Your system, subsystem, and integration testing, in other words, can begin on day one of system development.

STRUCTURED WALK-THRUS

In my estimation, a structured tool that rates a 10 on the usefulness scale (on a scale of 1 to 9) is structured walk-thrus.

I believe, for the time spent, structured walk-thrus give the most pay-back the soonest.

I have also seen that poorly run walk-thrus can cause untold damage to the people and productivity of a data processing shop.

Due to poorly run walk-thrus, I have seen:

A) a senior programmer/analyst fired
B) a programmer/analyst quit
C) a fight (using fists, even)
D) arguments that lasted for days
E) a walk-thru that lasted 6 hours, with <u>nothing</u> accomplished.

Therefore, the structured tool with potentially the most pay-back is also potentially the most dangerous.

A program walk-thru, in its simplest form, is merely looking at someone else's code and telling him/her what's wrong with it (it's obvious now why this tool is so bloody).

Walk-thrus have been called ego-less programming, which means it is an attempt to divorce the programmer's ego from the program (I created it; therefore, it's <u>mine</u>). I worked with a programmer once who was lured away to a different job via a head-hunter. A couple of days after he left, we had cause to use the source listings and documentation on one of the programs he had written. After several hours of searching, we not only came up empty-handed on that particular program (fortunately, we found the source and object code on our disk libraries) but it became apparent that all of the hard-copy documentation was missing for the projects he had worked on over the years. We chased him halfway across the midwest and spent considerable time convincing him that the stuff he had taken with him was not his. (I think he still believes it was.)

Once you have separated the programmer's ego from the program (which, of course, you can't do completely), you are then in a position to reap the real rewards of structured walk-thrus; namely, uncovering and correcting format errors and logic errors.

Since this is a painful process for most programmers, I would suggest applying some of the following guidelines for successful program walk-thrus.

1) Most of the walk-thru effort should be at the design (VTOC) level. You will find bugs are easier to see pictorially (VTOC) than in narrative form (COBOL). In addition, why code bugs?

Then when the coding begins, you just insure that the code follows the VTOC.

2) Only two subjects should be discussed in a walk-thru.

   a) Is the logic correct?
   b) Does the format of the code follow the standards? (To be discussed later.)

-- Notice: not included in "subjects to be discussed" are statements like "I know a better way to do it" or "Man, this sure is a stupid way of doing it" or "Why go to all that trouble when you can just ... ."

3) The first walk-thrus you attempt should include an outside moderator. This person should have no vested interest in the proceedings and be either a) extremely tough (so no one will mess with him/her) or b) extremely (pick one): pretty, handsome, loveable, innocent (so no one will want to mess with him/her). After the initial shock of walk-thrus have worn off, you may "dispose" of the outside moderator and the programmers themselves can become the moderators.

4) Hand out the material to be ~~walked-on~~ walked-thru at least 24 hours in advance.

5) One to three participants are all you need.

   a) Never invite your boss or your boss's boss (stick to your peers). Walk-thrus are meant to catch errors, not evaluate the programmer.

   b) The Systems Analyst who designed the subsystem your program is in would make a good participant.

6) In conducting the walk-thru, the programmer can first ask each individual what they found; and secondly, walk them through the logic explaining what is happening.

7) Never make any comment about the programmer - - - stick to the program.

Don't say "Look what you did here ... ."

                or

       "Why can't you ...?"

                or

       "Good grief turkey, can't you get it right?"

Instead, use comments about the program like:

       "I think this might be a problem."

                or

       "I can't understand the logic here."

8) Always have one positive thing to say about the program. (Even if it is just "This is sure good quality paper" or "You have spelled your name correctly, again!)

9) Participants should come prepared. Unprepared walk-thruees cause long walk-thrus. Once you get the hang of walk-thrus, they shouldn't last more than ten or fifteen minutes.

A well organized walk-thru program has a side benefit. Programmer trainees, that have constant input from their more experienced peers in walk-thrus, will become productive much sooner than they would if they were left on their own. A trainee working in the environment of a structured shop becomes productive much sooner than a trainee learning in an unstructured environment.

I once confirmed this by digging out a copy of a program I wrote after two years' experience in COBOL. L.K., who was a trainee programmer of about six months in a structured shop I worked in, gave me a program she had just finished. The "after six months" program developed in the structured shop was so superior to the "after two years" version developed in a "here's a COBOL manual" shop, it was embarrassing.

There are basically two types of walk-thrus: formal and informal.

Formal walk-thrus would adhere closely to the guide lines above. I would use formal walk-thrus for any new project program or major change.

Of course, a lot of programming involves small, quick, and dirty (usually more dirty than quick) changes to a program. Usually such changes never work the first time and considerable amount of time is spent trying to figure out what was overlooked.

It is amazing how many "oversights" can be caught before going into production by letting one other person do a quick perusal of the change to see if you overlooked something. A few minutes of explanation, a different perspective, and the majority of the maintenance bugs can be caught.

The further up the development cycle walk-thrus are applied (i.e. during analysis and design) the more effective they are. But if the programming phase is all that you have control over, they are still very useful.

At the coding level of development, structured testing and structured walk-thrus work very well together.

Assuming the VTOC is complete and has been walked-thru, a vigorous application of structured testing and walk-thrus might look like the following:

1) Code level A

2) Stub level B

3) Get a clean compile

4) Get one or two extra copies

5) Give a copy to the walk-thru attendees 24 hours in advance

6) Walk-thru level A (logic errors, format errors)

7) Make corrections

8) Test level A

9) Repeat this process dropping a level until arriving at the last level.

If you see the need to implement some of the structured tools throughout your shop, and if you have the authority to do so, and if you attempt
to do so like the majority of structured advocates, you will:

1) Write (or have someone write) a standards manual, next you will
2) Have several copies printed, then
3) Distribute them to all computer service people, and finally
4) Never hear another word about your manual or have anyone use it.

The only variation to this scenario is if you are really persistent
in getting everyone to adhere to your standards manual between steps 3 and
4, there will evolve huge battles between the authors of the manual and
the users.

Users: "This doesn't work in our environment."

Authors: "We have statistics to prove that it does."

Users: "It will slow us down."

Authors: "It will speed up development and we can prove it."

Users: "I have been writing code for 20 years."

Authors: "It's about time you wrote it correctly."

User: "I'll quit first."

Authors: "We can't help that."

Users: "There are too many rules and regulations - - you will
              curtail creativity."

Authors: "We must become more scientific and less artistic in our
              programs."

User: "Structured programming is inefficient on our computer."

Authors: "Hardware is cheap, we'll just add more."

I believe you need a "manual" to control the quality of your software.
I also believe the way you go about implementing your "standards manual"
is as important as its contents.

A few tips:

1) Get input and participation from those being affected by the
   standards.

2) In fact, let them develop their own standards.

3) Along with structured methods, you should include coding conventions in your manual. Coding conventions (what we have been calling the "format of the code") could include indentation rules, descriptive data names, matching IFs with ELSEs, comments on compound IFs, line up PIC clauses, use EJECTs and SKIPs and whatever makes your source listing easy to read.

4) Establish a "Standards committee" with members from all functions of your shop. Make your standards dynamic with a clear method of changing existing standards, include this method in the manual.

5) Enforcing standards is tougher than developing them. Include the method of enforcement in the standards manual.

POTPOURRI   (A few things to remember when implementing new tools.)

A) When applying any new tool, you will encounter a learning curve.

B) Structured methodologies force you to put the work up front (before coding).

C) There is no such thing as good, useful documentation (by documentation I mean something that is tacked on after the system is developed). The best documentation is the pictorial tools used to develop the system.

D) The higher up you go on the development cycle with structured tools, the more your productivity will increase.

    MIS - Business System Planning (BSP)
          Critical Success Factors (CSF)

    STRUCTURED ANALYSIS - Data flow diagrams (DFD), Data Dictionary

    STRUCTURED DESIGN - Structure charts, VTOC

    STRUCTURED PROGRAMMING - VTOC, HIPO, 6 Rules, Structured Testing

    STRUCTURED IMPLEMENTATION

    STRUCTURED MAINTENANCE

E) There are other good structured programming tools: Decision tables, Nassi-Schneiderman charts, Warnier diagrams, Bohm-Jacopini structures.

F) The higher up you go on the development cycle the higher up you have to go on the organizational chart for support.

G) Any tool has to be tailored to the particular environment. (E.g., some shops don't like levels in their COBOL code. They put the performed paragraph next to the performing paragraph.)

H) Getting started:

1) Pick a well-defined, high chance of success project or program.
2) Use only the programmers who want to give it a try.
3) Give all the techniques we have used a try.
4) Throw out what you do not think is worthwhile.
5) If other programmers laugh at you, remember Noah.